I0454867

U.S Fish & Wildlife Service

Mourning Dove *(Zenaida macroura)* Harvest and Population Parameters Derived from a National Banding Study

Biological Technical Publication

BTP-R3010-2008

David L. Otis[1]

John H. Schulz[2]

David P. Scott[3]

[1] U.S. Geological Survey, Iowa Cooperative Fish and Wildlife Research Unit, Iowa State University, Ames, IA
[2] Missouri Department of Conservation, Columbia, MO
[3] Ohio Division of Wildlife, Columbus, OH

Author contact information:
David L. Otis
U.S. Geological Survey
Iowa Cooperative Fish and Wildlife Research Unit
342 Science II
Iowa State University
Ames, IA 50011
Phone: (515) 294-7639
E-mail: dotis@iastate.edu

John H. Schulz
Resource Science Center
Missouri Department of Conservation
1110 South College Avenue
Columbia, Missouri 65201
Phone: (573) 882-9909
E-mail: John.H.Schulz@mdc.mo.gov

David P. Scott
Ohio Department of Natural Resources
Division of Wildlife
2045 Morse Road, Building G
Columbus, OH 43229
Phone: (614) 265-6338
E-mail: Dave.Scott@dnr.state.oh.us

For additional copies or information, contact:
David L. Otis
U.S. Geological Survey
Iowa Cooperative Fish and Wildlife Research Unit
342 Science II
Iowa State University
Ames, IA 50011
Phone: (515) 294-7639
E-mail: dotis@iastate.edu

Recommended citation:
Otis, D. L., J. H. Schulz, and D. P. Scott. 2008.
Mourning Dove (*Zenaida macroura*) harvest and
population parameters derived from a national
banding study. U.S. Department of Interior,
Fish and Wildlife Service, Biological Technical
Publication FWS/BTP-R3010-2008, Washington,
D.C.

Series Senior Technical Editor:
Stephanie L. Jones
Fish and Wildlife Service
Region 6 Nongame Migratory Bird Coordinator
P.O. Box 25486
Denver Federal Center
Denver, Colorado 80225-0486

Table of Contents

List of Figures

List of Tables

Executive Summary

The Mourning Dove (*Zenaida macroura; dove)* is the most harvested migratory game bird in North America and a ubiquitous species that is valued and easily recognized by the general public. Informed harvest management of this important recreational resource requires knowledge of harvest attributes and population vital rates, several of which are estimable from banding and from hunter-harvested birds. We conducted a national-scale banding program in 2003 – 2005 to generate such data for estimation of band reporting rates, harvest rates, distribution and derivation of harvest, and annual survival rates. The study required training of a new cadre of biologists in field techniques and establishment of data collection and management protocols, as well as providing an opportunity to evaluate logistics and costs associated with the large-scale study design.

During 2003 – 2005, biologists in 29 participating states banded nearly 100,000 birds, and hunters have reported almost 5,000 bands to date from harvested doves. In 2004 and 2005, a proportion of the trapped and released doves received an extra reward band which allowed estimation of the probability that a hunter reported a band from a harvested dove to the United States Geological Survey Bird Banding Laboratory. This reporting rate varied considerably among geographic regions (range: 0.40 – 0.85). Weighted average adult harvest rates for the Eastern Management Unit ($\bar{x}$ = 0.074 ± SE = 0.002) and Central Management Unit ($\bar{x}$ = 0.062 ± SE = 0.004) were similar. Adult harvest rates were greatest in the Western Management Unit ($\bar{x}$ = 0.091 ± SE = 0.003), but this estimate was influenced by the single large estimate from California in 2005. Juvenile harvest rates were greatest in the Eastern Management Unit ($\bar{x}$ = 0.095 ± SE = 0.002) and similar in the Central Management Unit ($\bar{x}$ = 0.071 ± SE = 0.003) and Western Management Unit ($\bar{x}$ = 0.064 ± SE = 0.003). With the exception of only a few states in the northern U.S., at least 80% of the harvest of banded adults and juveniles occurred in the state of banding. Similarly, with only a few exceptions, nearly all recoveries in each state were derived from banded cohorts in the same state.

Average adult subregion survival rates ($\bar{S}$ = 0.350, range = 0.261 - 0.732) were generally greater than corresponding subregion juvenile survival rates ($\bar{S}$ = 0.370, range = 0.153 - 0.385).

Comparison to results from reporting rate studies conducted more than 30 years ago suggests a large average increase in reporting rate, probably due to the availability of the Bird Banding Laboratory toll-free telephone number for reporting bands. The last national-scale dove banding study was conducted more than 30 years ago, and a comparison of harvest rates suggests current harvest rate estimates for both age classes in Eastern Management Unit and Western Management Unit states are generally less than previous estimates, while estimates are greater or about the same in Central Management Unit states. Survival rates from the earlier study were significantly greater for both age classes in the Eastern Management Unit and the Central Management Unit (P ≤ 0.10), but no differences were found in the Western Management Unit. We did not find any important changes in harvest distribution or derivation patterns within the management units.

This study provided the foundation for an operational long-term banding program that is critical to the implementation of the National Mourning Dove Strategic Harvest Management Plan (Anonymous 2005), which describes the conceptual framework for an improved, informed system of harvest management for doves.

Acknowledgments

We thank the U.S. Fish and Wildlife Service Webless Migratory Game Bird Research Program, a consortium of state wildlife agencies, and Texas Parks and Wildlife Department for funding. We are indebted to the hundreds of people who did the hard work of banding birds and the state coordinators who organized these efforts in their respective states (see Appendix C). We thank Pam Garretson for assistance with training and technical support of Band Manager software, and David Dolton for administrative and technical support of this project. Billy Dukes and Bill Harvey provided valuable comments on a first draft of the manuscript, and Jim Dubovsky, Steve Hayslette, Nova Silvy and one anonymous reviewer provided excellent subsequent peer review. We thank Carol Petticord, the Wildlife Management Institute, Graham Smith, and the U.S Geological Survey Patuxent Wildlife Research Center for assistance in budget management. The U.S Geological Survey Bird Banding Laboratory provided essential staff support for logistics of the reward banding effort and assistance with data management. We thank the many students at Iowa State University who spent days in the basement creating data forms and stringing bands, with special thanks to Josh Obrecht for managing student help and generating maps and graphics. We thank Jenny Loda for additional assistance with graphics. The Iowa Cooperative Fish and Wildlife Research Unit is supported by a cooperative agreement between the U.S. Geological Survey, Iowa State University, the Iowa Department of Natural Resources, and the Wildlife Management Institute.

Introduction

The Mourning Dove (*Zenaida macroura; dove*) is currently classified as a migratory game bird in 38 of the lower 48 states. It is the most widespread, abundant, and harvested migratory game bird in North America, and its popularity as a game species is confirmed by the fact that > 1.1 million hunters participate in dove hunting each year (Dolton and Rau 2006). Annual hunting regulations are established by the U.S. Fish and Wildlife Service (FWS), after consideration of input from technical committees and flyway councils that represent each of the 3 dove management units (MUs): Eastern (EMU), Central (CMU) and Western (WMU) (Fig. 1).

Informed harvest management strategies for migratory game birds depend upon knowledge of population dynamics and how the harvest process affects these dynamics. This knowledge depends, in turn, on reliable estimates of critical demographic vital rates, harvest parameters and population status at appropriate temporal and spatial scales. Historically, large-scale monitoring and survey programs for doves have been very limited. The primary monitoring effort has been the Call-Count Survey (CCS), which is an annual roadside survey coordinated since 1966 by the FWS to index breeding population trends nationwide. The Harvest Information Program (HIP) is an annual FWS mail survey of hunters that was fully implemented in 2002 (Ver Steeg and Elden 2002) and produces estimates of national dove harvest and hunter effort. The last national banding study was conducted by federal and state agencies for several years beginning in the mid-1960s. Although a national-scale experimental wing collection survey to estimate harvest age ratios was begun in 2005 (Otis and Miller, pers. comm.), a large-scale annual recruitment survey has not yet been established.

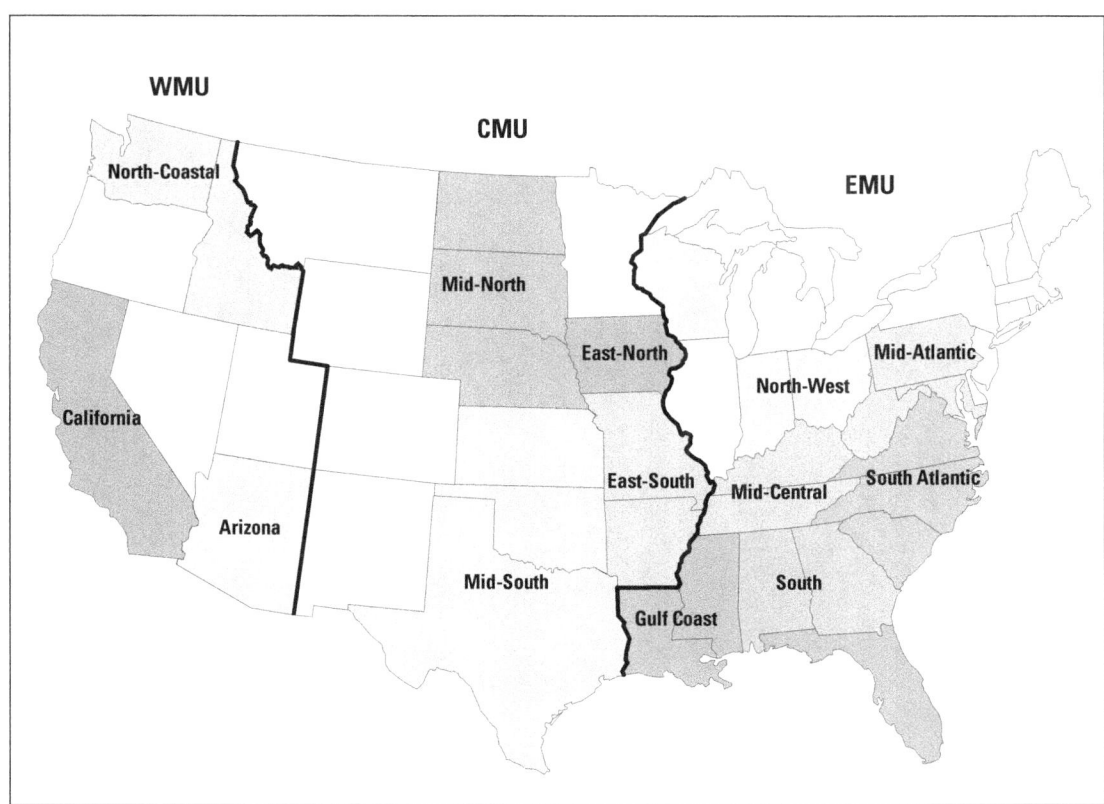

Figure 1. Map of participating States, with Management Unit boundaries (━━━) and subregion (EMU: Eastern Management Unit, CMU: Central Management Unit, WMU: Western Management Unit).

In 1999, new initiatives were begun within the dove management community based on a desire for improved, science-based harvest strategies for dove populations. In 2003, these efforts culminated in the approval of the Mourning Dove National Strategic Harvest Management Plan (National Plan; Anonymous 2005) by the flyway councils and the International Association of Fish and Wildlife Agencies.

Knowledge of population harvest rate is essential for informed management of exploited species (Sadler 1993). For migratory birds, band-recovery studies are used to estimate recovery rates, i.e., the proportion of a banded cohort that is shot, retrieved, and reported to the U.S. Geological Survey Bird Banding Laboratory (BBL). Recovery rates are often used as an index to harvest rate, but these indices are lower than true harvest rates because not all recovered bands are reported to the BBL. Harvest rate estimates are obtained by adjusting recovery rates by the reporting rate, i.e., the probability that a hunter reports the band number from a harvested banded bird. Reporting rates can be estimated by use of reward bands, which are similar to standard metal bands placed on birds, but inscribed with a dollar value that will be paid to the individual who reports the band. By comparing recovery rates of birds banded with standard bands only to those banded with both standard and reward bands, we can derive reporting rate estimates, assuming that the reward amount is sufficient to insure that a hunter will report the band number (Nichols and Tomlinson 1993, Nichols et al. 1995). Previous reward-band studies for Mourning Doves were conducted on a limited geographic scale by Tomlinson (1968), Reeves (1979), and Scott et al. (2004), but a national-scale effort has never been conducted. Recent changes in the band-reporting mechanism from a mail to toll-free telephone system, as well as potential changes in hunter behavior, also motivated the need for this study.

This banding study was a cooperative effort between state wildlife agencies and the FWS Division of Migratory Bird Management, and was initiated as the first tangible effort to implement a dove harvest strategy envisioned in the National Plan (Anonymous 2005). We conducted the study in 29 states (Fig. 1) during 2003 – 2005. Funds from the FWS Webless Migratory Game Bird Research Program were used to pay band rewards and to cover administrative, coordination, and reporting requirements. Cooperating state wildlife agencies, supplemented in some states by assistance from FWS personnel and private citizens, conducted the banding program. Agency participation was strictly voluntary.

Objectives

The primary objective of this study was to estimate reporting rate and age-specific harvest rates in a representative set of states in each of the 3 dove management units. These units (Fig. 1) were delineated by Kiel (1959) based on examination of band recovery data. Secondary objectives were to use the band-recovery data to describe the spatial distribution and derivation of harvest and to estimate annual age-specific survival rates (Brownie et al. 1985). In addition, we intended to use the experience gained in training of field personnel, establishment of data collection and management protocols, and assessment of required costs, to help guide the design and implementation of a future operational nationwide banding program.

Methods

Field Methods

We trapped doves in 29 states (Fig. 1) between 1 July and 15 August using standard modified Kniffin funnel traps (Reeves et al. 1968) and a variety of small grain baits. We classified banded birds as After Hatching Year (adult), Hatching Year (juvenile) or Unknown (Mirarchi 1993, Schulz et al. 1995). Gender cannot reliably be assigned to juveniles and therefore all were classified as unknown; adult birds were classified as male, female, or unknown (Mirarchi 1993, Schulz et al. 1995). The band type (standard) was a FWS metal butt-end band inscribed with the BBL address and a toll-free phone number, either of which could be used to report the band to the BBL.

Banding Scheme

2003. No reward bands were deployed in 2003 based on the rationale that the first year of banding provided the opportunity for participating states to establish banding locations, train personnel in trapping techniques and age and gender assignment, standardize data collection and management protocols, and evaluate field costs. We conducted workshops for state banding coordinators in each management unit to discuss and finalize these details, and most state coordinators subsequently conducted similar workshops within their own state.

Due to concern about the detectability of standard bands on harvested birds, 50% of birds banded in 2003 received an unnumbered gold-colored band in addition to a standard band. The concern arose from two considerations: 1) no large-scale dove banding program had been conducted for 30 years; thus hunters are not conditioned to look for bands on harvested birds, and 2) the small band size and aluminum color of a standard band could result in failure to see the band. Comparison of recovery rates of the two marked cohorts provided a check on the assumption that detectability of bands did not confound estimates of reporting rate.

2004. Reward bands were deployed in all 29 participating states in 2004. We placed only a standard band on all adult birds. In addition to a standard band, we placed a reward band on the opposite leg of every third juvenile bird. We placed reward bands only on juvenile birds because of their greater vulnerability to harvest (Dunks et al. 1982), which would result in larger sample sizes for

estimation of reporting rates. The reward amount was $100, which was considered sufficient to satisfy the critical assumption that a hunter would report a reward band with near certainty (Nichols et al. 1995, Royle and Garrettson, unpubl. data). We assumed that reporting rates would not vary among age or gender cohorts, because these characteristics cannot be reliably identified for birds in flight, nor do we believe hunters preferentially value one cohort over another.

2005. The initial study design specified that only standard bands would be used in 2005. However, we did supplemental reward banding in several states (ND, SD, NE, KS, OK, TX, AZ) based on a desire to improve statistical precision of reporting rate estimates derived from the 2004 data. California joined the study in 2005 and also deployed reward bands.

Field Design and Banding Quotas

The National Plan (Anonymous 2005) suggested continuation of the practice of setting harvest regulations by MU, and this was considered the highest level of aggregation for the results. Due to uncertainty about the potential costs to the participating states for training and fieldwork, we assigned banding quotas to subregions (1 or more states) within each MU (Fig. 1). Our EMU subregion boundaries had been used in prior analyses of dove banding studies (Hayne and Geissler 1977, Otis 2002, 2003). We used the longitudinal boundaries defined by Dunks et al. (1982) and Tomlinson et al. (1988) and, in consultation with expert federal and state dove biologists, we added an additional mid-latitudinal boundary to define CMU and WMU subregions boundaries (Fig. 1). Groups of states within subregions cooperated to achieve banding quota objectives. We allocated the state quotas within the subregion in proportion to their area and average 1997 – 2001 CCS population index. In multi-state subregions with only a single state participant (e.g., EMU – North-West, CMU – East-North; Fig. 1), we arbitrarily assigned the state 50% of the subregion quota.

Given the objective of 1) a standard error of 5% for the reporting rate in each subregion, 2) an expected reporting rate of 30%, and 3) an expected average harvest rate of 10%, standard statistical calculations suggested the best ratio of reward bands to standard bands was approximately 1:2, with subregion quotas of 1,000 birds of each age-class in 2003 and 2005, and 1,000 adult, 700 juvenile (reward + standard) and 1,400 juvenile (standard only) birds in 2004. States that conducted supplemental reward banding in 2005 used 2004 quotas. With the exception of juvenile birds in reward banding states and years, all states were free to band in excess of their assigned quotas.

We used a 3-step process to choose banding locations. We stratified the subregion into 1-degree latitude by 1-degree longitude blocks. These blocks averaged about 100 km x 100 km. Each subregion had at least 30 degree blocks, and the design objective was to band in a representative sample of 20 blocks. If not all states in a subregion were participating, then the number of banding degree blocks was reduced accordingly. Each state biologist was free to choose these blocks based on their knowledge of dove populations, hunting pressure and available resources. Within each of these blocks, biologists also were responsible for choosing specific banding sites.

Data Analysis

Data Sources
Banding. — Numbers of birds banded in each age and sex cohort for each state and year were derived from electronic spreadsheets provided to us by state banding coordinators. We used a standard template developed by the FWS for data entry, processing, and interface with BBL Band Manager software.

Recoveries. — We used recovery data from the 2003-2005 hunting seasons provided by the BBL in May 2006. We used recoveries only from birds banded by study participants. We used only recoveries from birds shot and retrieved by hunters, which comprised > 95% of the total recoveries of all types.

Parameter Estimations
Reporting Rates. — For each state, we combined all birds banded during the study and calculated the percentage of recoveries that occurred in that state. If this percentage was ≥ 80%, we estimated a reporting rate for the state using only these recoveries. This 80% recovery criterion was met in all states except OK and TX. Reporting rates could not be calculated for IA, since it is a non-hunting state, nor for WI and IN because they did not deploy reward bands. We used Program SURVIV (White 1983) to estimate reporting rates and standard errors for the "> 80%" states. The reporting rate was assumed to be constant across years and age-classes. The estimation models also included age-specific annual survival rates (assumed constant across years) and harvest rates (age- and year-specific); these estimates are discussed below. Also, models contained an additional parameter to adjust for a different reporting rate for 2003 birds equipped with the extra blank gold band. Direct (banded birds recovered in the first hunting season following banding) and indirect (banded birds recovered in subsequent hunting seasons) recoveries were used in the models. In a few states, some year/age cohorts

were eliminated from models because of small sample sizes.

For states that did not meet the 80% criterion, we estimated reporting rates by adapting the Program SURVIV models used by Nichols et al. (1995). For OK, we used recoveries from birds banded in AR, KS and OK; for TX we used recoveries from birds banded in IA, KS, OK, SD and TX. Because CA banded only in 2005, we estimated reporting rate using standard formulas (Nichols and Tomlinson 1993).

We estimated subregion reporting rates by calculating a weighted average of estimates from states within the subregion. Similarly, we estimated the management unit rate by calculating a weighted average over all states within the unit. State weights were proportional to the average state HIP harvest estimates from 2003 - 2005.

Harvest Rates. — If at least 80% of the recoveries of both age-classes occurred in the state of banding, we used recoveries from all states of harvest in the same models described previously for reporting rate to estimate annual age-specific harvest rates. Similarly, harvest rates for OK and TX were estimated using the custom Program SURVIV models used for estimation of reporting rate. Harvest distributions for birds banded in WV, ND, SD, NE, KS and ID involved several states; therefore we estimated harvest rates by using state-specific direct recovery rates of standard bands and reporting rates for each state of harvest. We assigned the ID reporting rate to UT, OR and NM in the calculation of ID harvest rates. We assigned the OH reporting rate to IN and WI in the calculation of their harvest rates. We assigned a reporting rate of 0.25 to Mexico, which was used in the calculation of ND, SD, NE and KS harvest rates. We calculated weighted estimates for subregions and the management unit with state weights proportional to the product of the area of dove habitat in the state and its average 1996 – 2005 CCS index. The area of dove habitat for each state was taken from Kiel (1959). Because doves are habitat generalists and their breeding range includes the entire lower 48 states, the only appreciable difference between Kiel's dove habitat area and the total state area occurs in states with substantial mountain or woodland areas. In our study, these states were NC, PA, WV, WI, ID and WA.

Survival Rates. — Age-specific average annual survival rates were estimated for each state using Program SURVIV (White 1983) models with all harvest recoveries from cohorts banded in that state. Estimates could not be calculated for CA and WI because of only 1 year of banding data, and the estimate for IN is based on only 2 years of banding. We calculated estimates for subregions and the management unit as described for harvest rates.

Harvest Distribution and Derivation

Distribution. We estimated state harvest distribution, i.e., the set of percentages of the harvest recoveries from banded cohorts in a given state that occurred in each state of harvest (Munro and Kimball 1982), for each age-class and for all age-classes combined. Numbers of recoveries in each state were adjusted by the state reporting rate. Data were pooled over all years.

Derivation. We estimated the derivation of harvest for each state, i.e., the percentage of each state's harvest derived from all source banding states, by following a method described by Geis (1972) and Dunks et al. (1982). Data were pooled over all years. The estimates weighted each recovery from a source state by the relative population abundance that it represented. We calculated the source state weight (W) as

$$W = \frac{\text{(state dove habitat area)*(median CCS index, 1996 – 2005)}}{\text{Number of birds banded in the source state}}$$

Weights were calculated separately for each age-class because the number of birds banded was different in each age-class.

Results

Banding

Nearly 100,000 doves were banded in the three MUs (EMU: 55% of total, CMU: 35% of total, WMU: 10% of total) during the three-year study (Fig. 2). Forty-two percent were adults, 56% were juveniles, and 2% were unknown age class. In the adult age class, 62% of banded doves were identified as males, 28% as females, and 10% as unknown gender. Approximately 8,000 birds were released with reward bands. State-, year-, and age-specific banding summaries are presented in Appendix A.

Recoveries

Nearly 5,000 recoveries were reported by hunters during the 2003 – 2005 hunting seasons. Direct recoveries comprised 80% of the total recoveries and approximately 60% of the direct recoveries were of juvenile birds. Approximately 60% of the 2003 recoveries had the additional blank gold band. State- and age-specific recovery summaries are presented in Appendix B.

Reporting Rates

Subregion reporting rates ranged from about 0.40 in AZ and the Mid-South to 0.85 in the Mid-North, and with an average = 0.55 (Fig. 3). Individual subregion estimates were moderately precise ($\overline{CV}$ = 19%). Average subregion estimates within each management unit were 0.53 (EMU), 0.57 (CMU) and 0.57 (WMU). Reporting rates for individual states (Table 1) were not as precise ($\overline{CV}$ = 28%) and ranged from about 0.30 (GA, OK, TX, WV) to 1.00 (ND, SD, ID).

Harvest Rates

Average state harvest rates varied by 10 to 18 percentage points among states within each of the three MUs (Tables 2a, 2b). There was relatively less annual variation within a state than spatial variation among states. Annual state harvest rate estimates were not precise ($\overline{CV}$ = 36%).

Average subregion harvest rates were slightly lower for adults ($\overline{x}$ = 0.069; range = 0.010 – 0.204) than juveniles ($\overline{x}$ = 0.079; range = 0.021 – 0.147; Fig. 4). There was generally small variation among years within subregions. Annual subregion estimates were

moderately precise ($\overline{CV}$ = 24%). Weighted average MU adult harvest rates were greatest in the WMU ($\overline{x}$ = 0.091 ± SE = 0.003), but this estimate was inflated by the single large estimate of 0.204 for CA in 2005. Adult harvest rates for the EMU ($\overline{x}$ = 0.074 ± SE = 0.002) and CMU ($\overline{x}$ = 0.062 ± SE = 0.004) were similar. Juvenile harvest rates were greatest in the EMU ($\overline{x}$ = 0.095 ± SE = 0.002) and similar in the CMU ($\overline{x}$ = 0.071 ± SE = 0.003) and WMU ($\overline{x}$ = 0.064 ± SE = 0.003).

Survival Rates

Individual state adult survival rates averaged about 15 percentage points greater than juvenile survival rates in the EMU and CMU, but were nearly equal in the WMU (Table 3). There was considerable variation between state age-specific survival rate estimates but these state estimates were very imprecise (adult $\overline{CV}$ = 32%; juvenile $\overline{CV}$ = 42%), and should therefore be interpreted with caution.

Subregion adult survival rates ranged from 0.261 in the EMU South to 0.732 in the CMU East-North (IA; Table 3; Fig. 5). Subregion juvenile survival rates ranged from 0.153 in the EMU Gulf Coast to 0.385 in the WMU North-Coastal. Subregion estimates were more precise than state estimates (adult $\overline{CV}$ = 22%; juvenile $\overline{CV}$ = 29%).

Harvest Distribution

A high percentage of the total number of recoveries from a state's adult ($\overline{x}$ = 87%) and juvenile ($\overline{x}$ = 80%) banded cohorts occurred in the state of banding (Table 4). Exceptions were the northern states of ND, NE and SD and ID, for which the percentage was 20 – 40 points less than average for adults. For juveniles in these states and in KS, the percentage was 25 – 65 points less than average. Adults banded in AZ, IA, ID, ND and TX, and juveniles banded in AR, CA, ID, KS, ND, NE, SD, TX and WA were recovered in Mexico (Table 4). Juveniles from the non-hunting state of IA were recovered from 13 different states and Mexico.

Harvest Derivation

Nearly all recoveries in each state were derived from banded cohorts in the same state. Harvest derivation calculations indicate that an average of 94% of the adult harvest was derived from a state's breeding population, and this percentage was at least 75% for all states (Table 5). For juveniles, the average was 92%, and only LA and TX fell slightly below 75%. Caution is necessary in the interpretation of these results, because of the bias caused by non-banding states. Clearly, there can be no contribution of a non-banding state in the derivation calculations for any other state, and thus the estimates are conditional upon the set of banding states. Also, we included derivation results for some non-banding states and Mexico, but in this case the contributions of banding states are obviously inflated because of the lack of banding in the state of harvest.

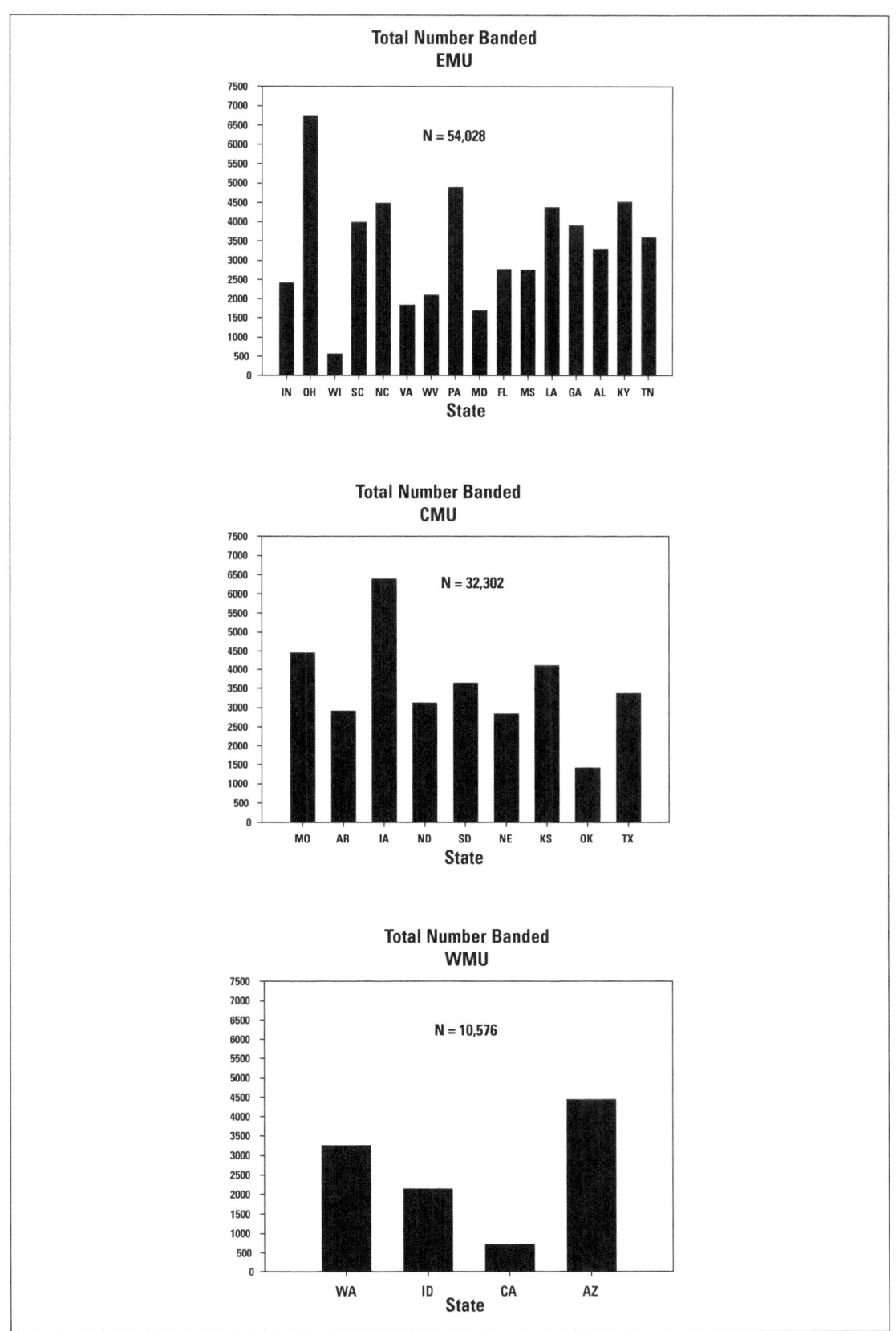

Figure 2. Numbers of Mourning Doves banded in each State and management unit (EMU: Eastern Management Unit, CMU: Central Management Unit, WMU: Western Management Unit), 2003 - 2005.

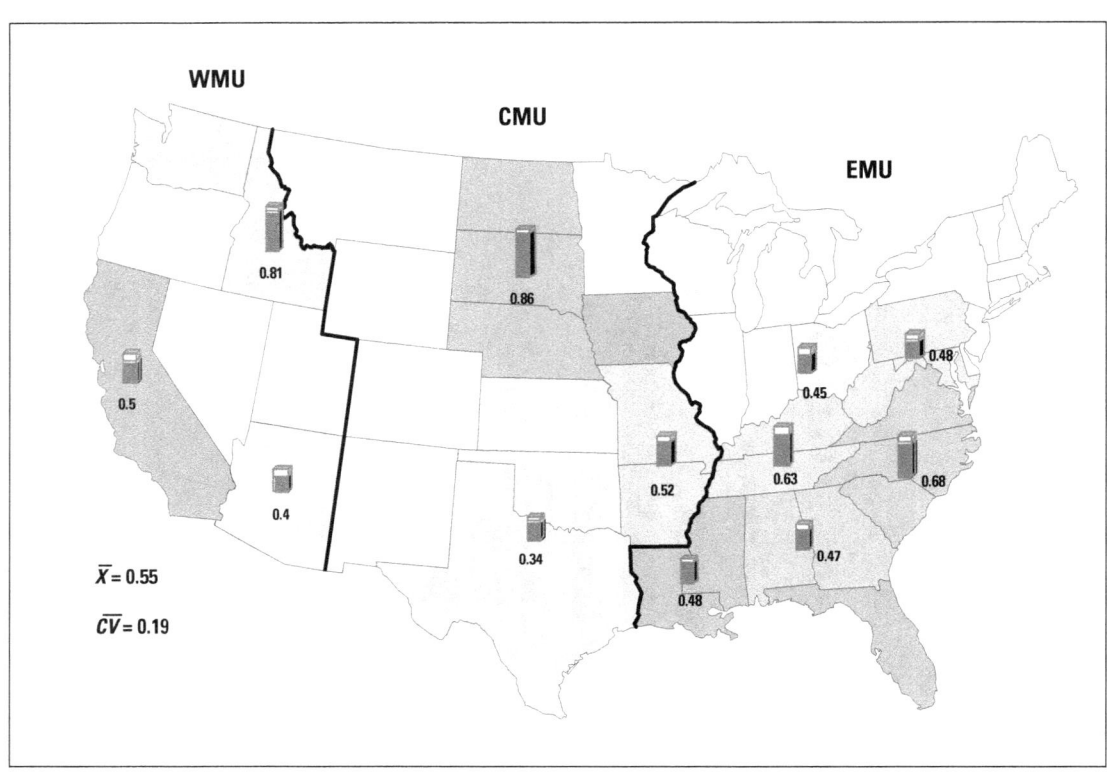

Figure 3. Mourning Dove reporting rates by subregions; CV is indicated by white portion of bar.

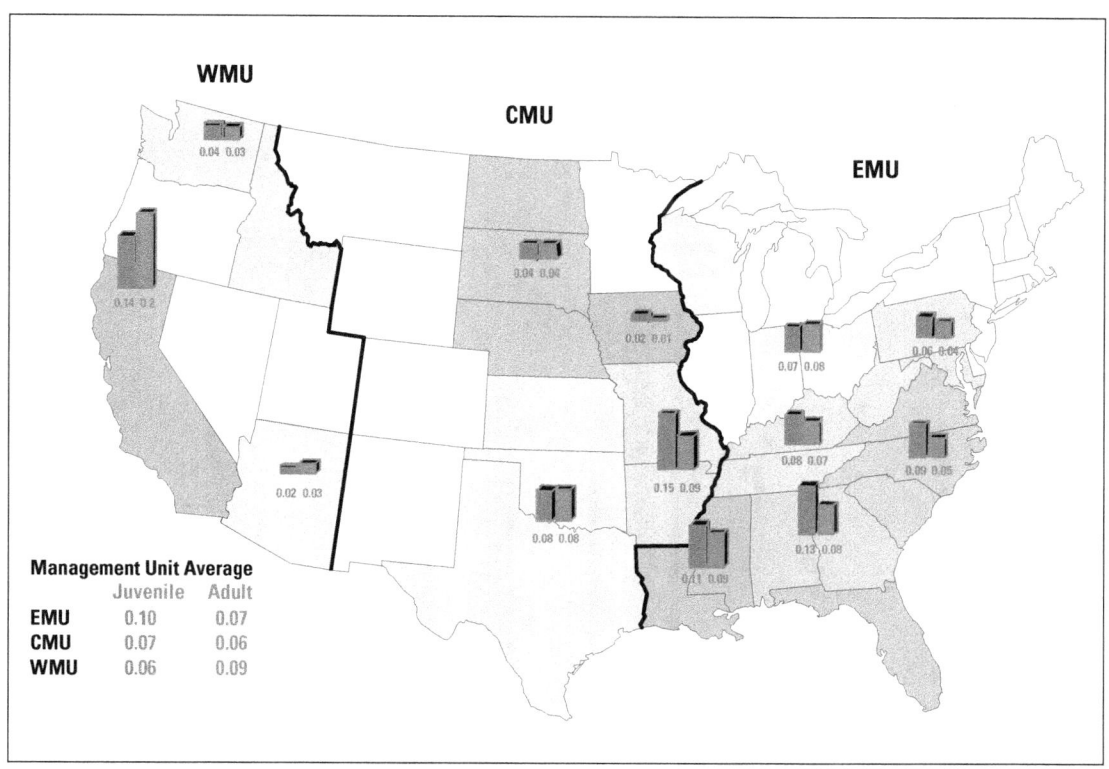

Figure 4. Average 2003 – 2005 Mourning Dove adult and juvenile harvest rates by subregion and management unit (EMU: Eastern Management Unit, CMU: Central Management Unit, WMU: Western Management Unit).

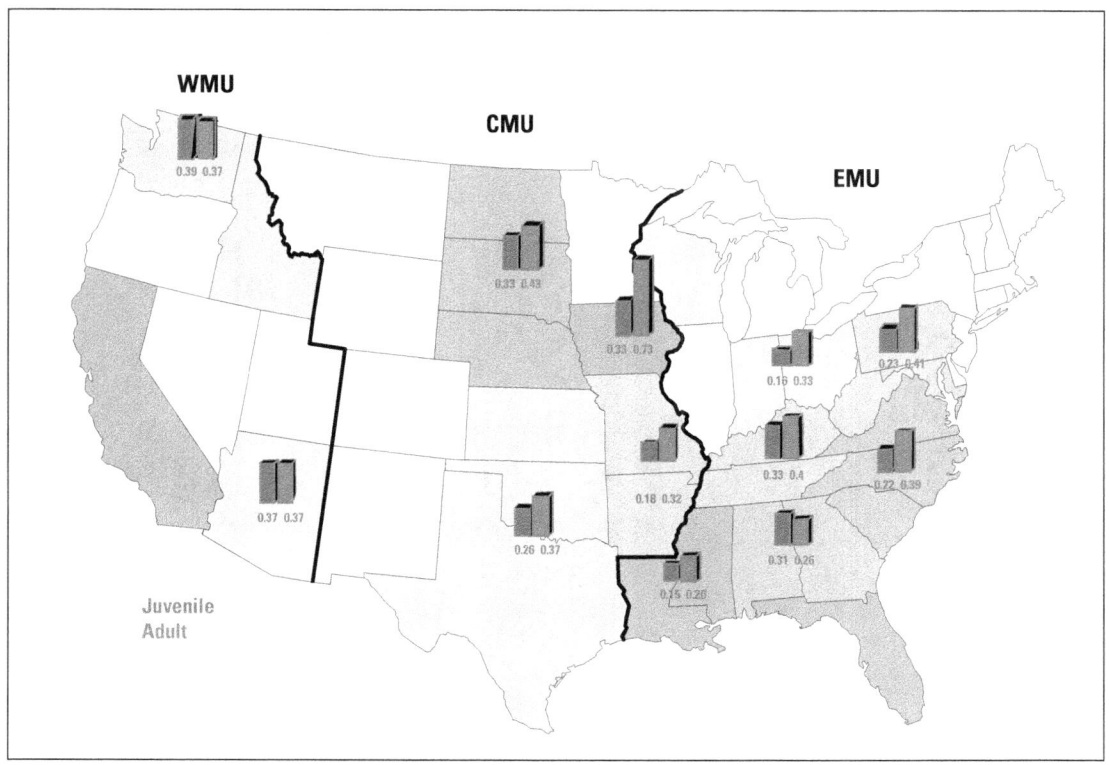

Figure 5. Adult and juvenile Mourning Dove survival rates by subregion for 2003 -2005.

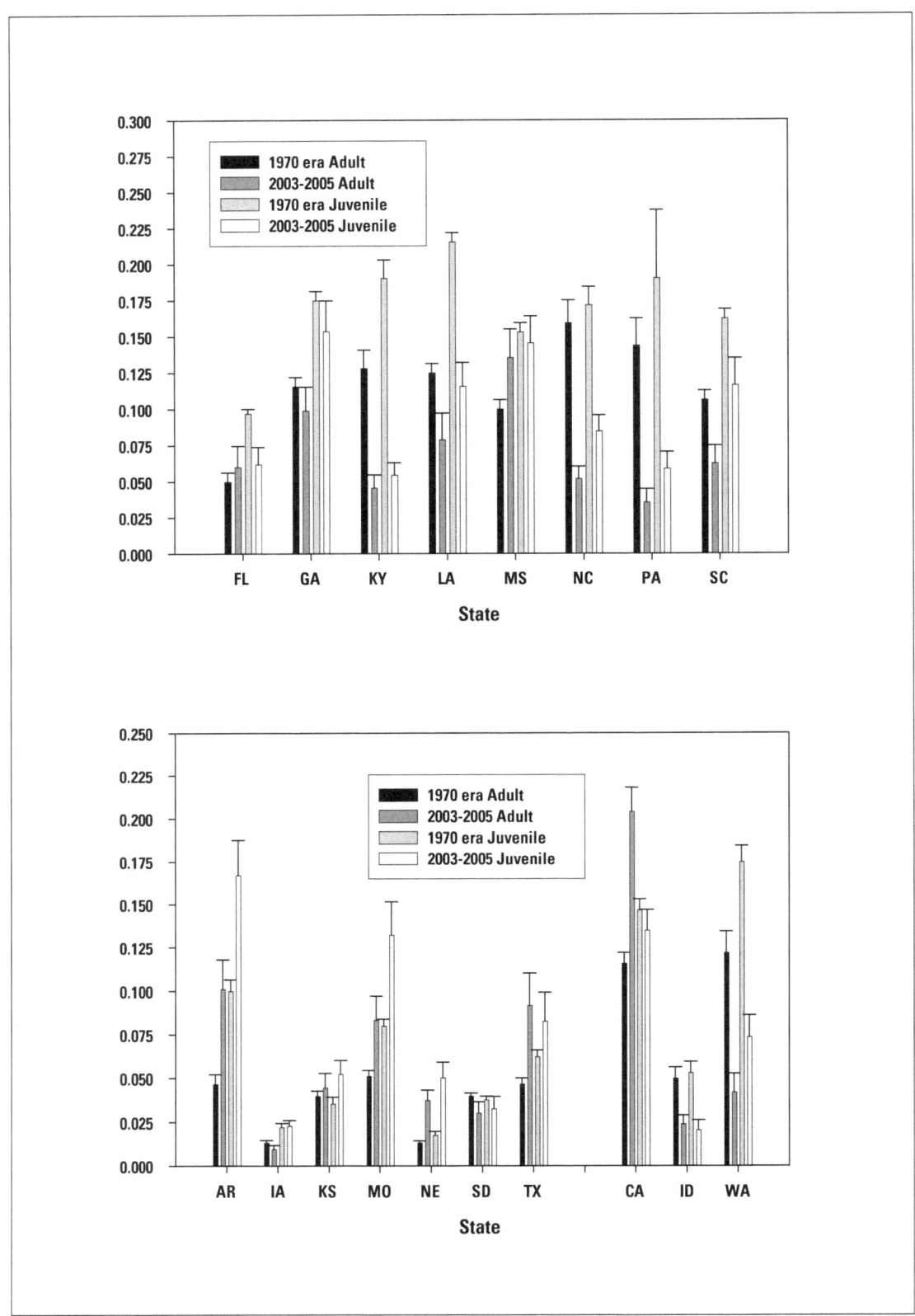

Figure 6. Comparison between 1970 era (1966 – 1971 (EMU States), 1967 – 1974 (CMU States), 1964 – 1974 (WMU States)) and 2003 – 2005 of average age-specific Mourning Dove harvest rate estimates (+ 1 SE) by State (EMU: Eastern Management Unit, CMU: Central Management Unit, WMU: Western Management Unit).

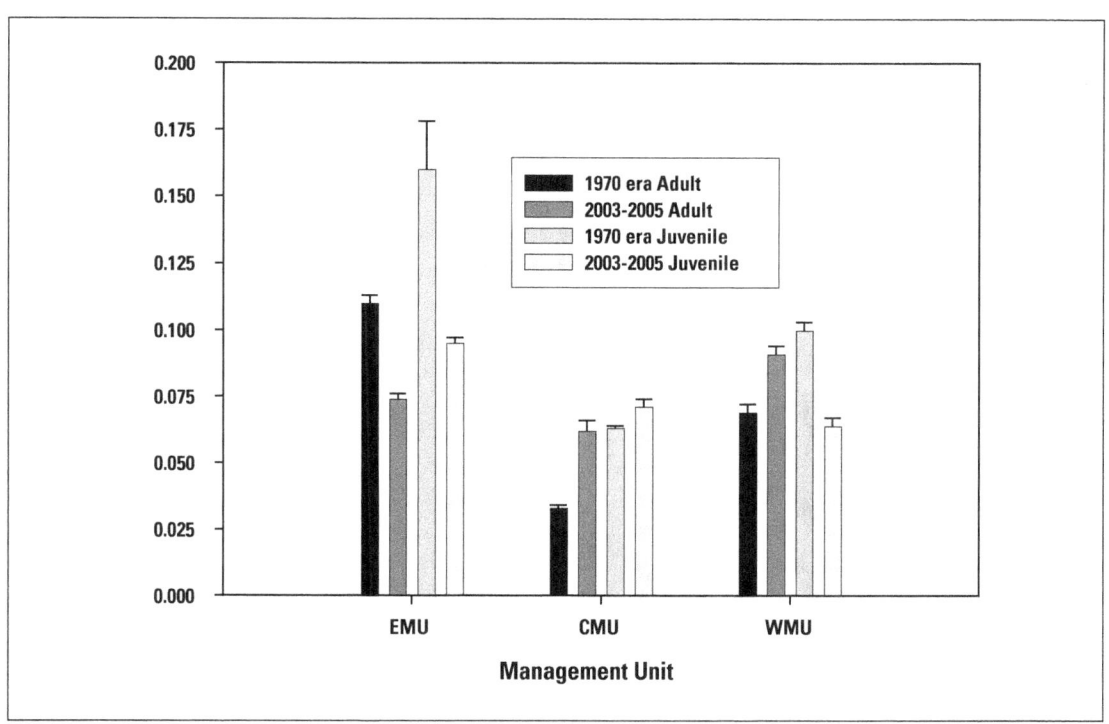

Figure 7. Comparison between 1970 era (1966 – 1971 (EMU), 1967 – 1974 (CMU), 1964 – 1974 (WMU)) and 2003 – 2005 of average age-specific Mourning Dove harvest rate estimates (+ 1 SE) by management unit (EMU: Eastern Management Unit, CMU: Central Management Unit, WMU: Western Management Unit).

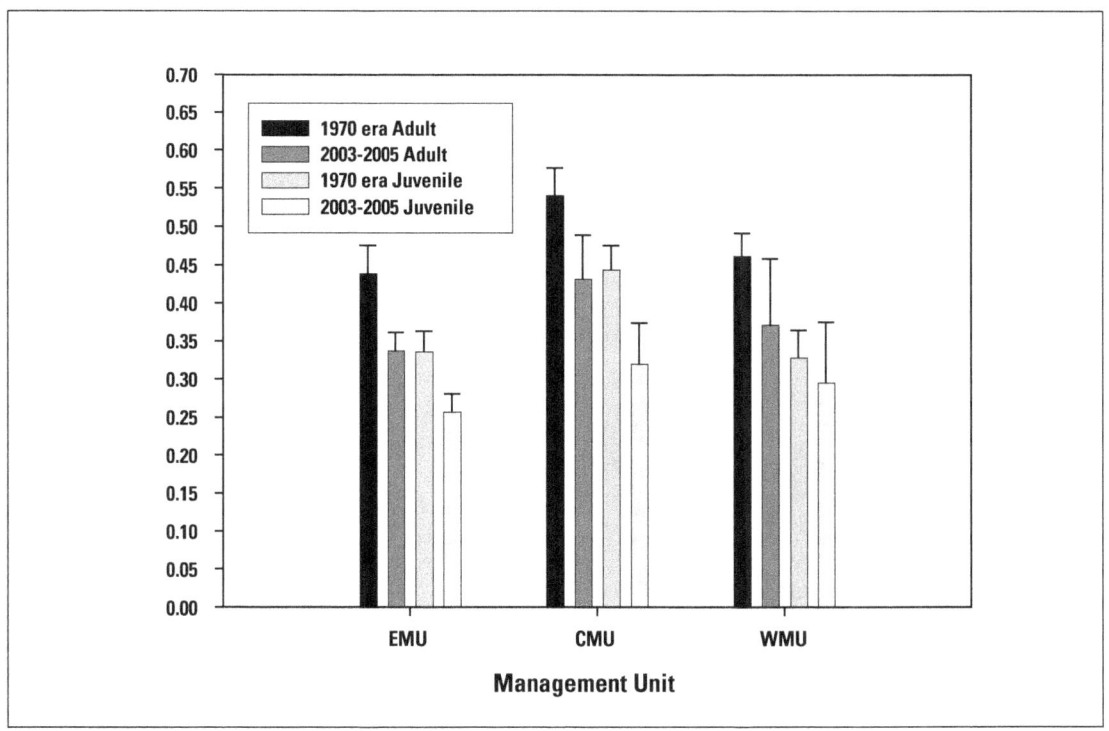

Figure 8. Comparison between 1970 era (1966 – 1971 (EMU subregions), 1967 – 1974 (CMU subregions), 1964 – 1975 (WMU subregions)) and 2003 – 2005 Mourning Dove age-specific survival rates (+ 1 SE) by subregion (EMU: Eastern Management Unit, CMU: Central Management Unit, WMU: Western Management Unit).

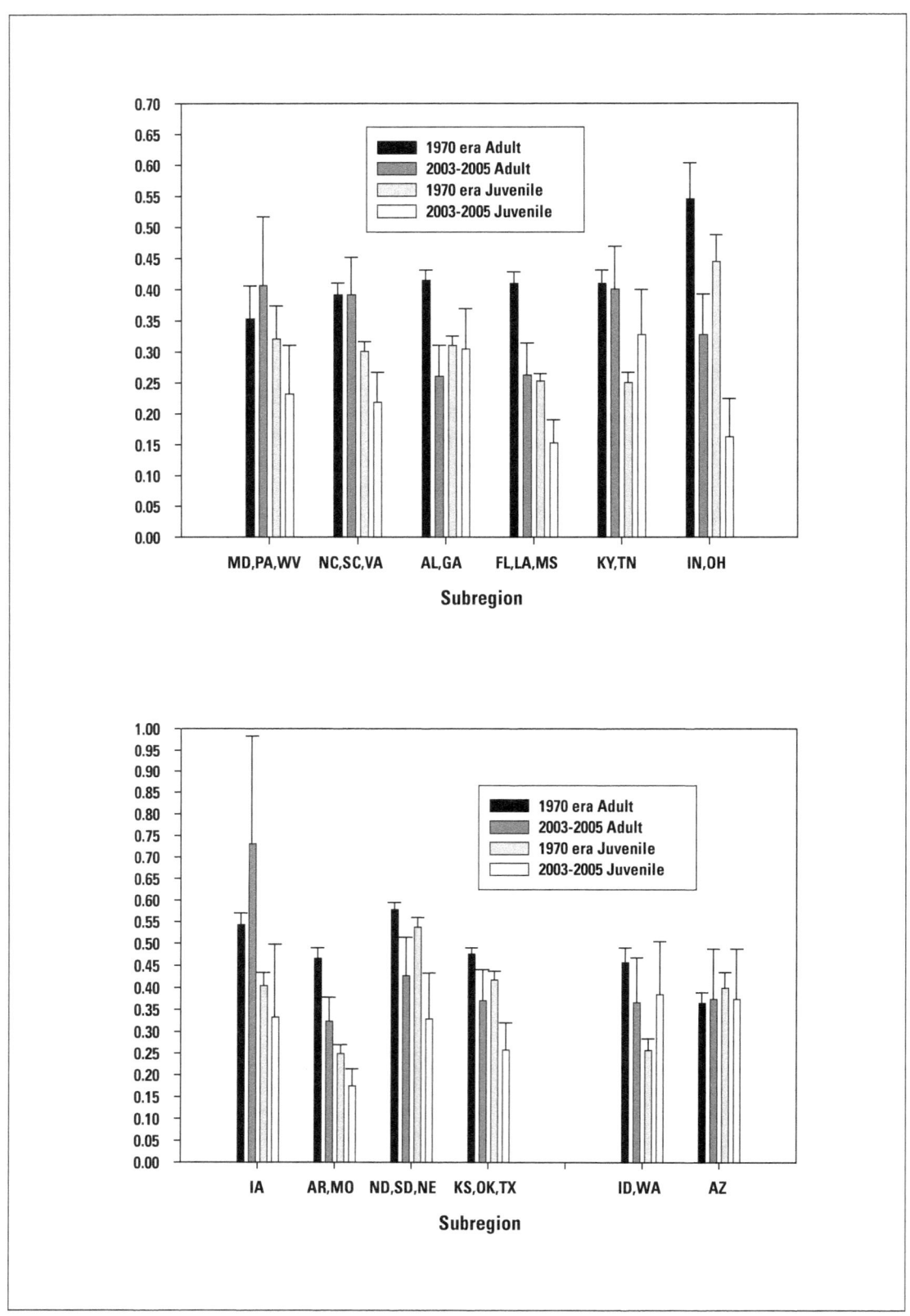

Figure 9. Comparison between 1970 era (1966 – 1971 (EMU), 1967 – 1974 (CMU), 1964 – 1975 (WMU)) and 2003 – 2005 Mourning Dove age-specific survival rates (+ 1 SE), by management unit (EMU: Eastern Management Unit, CMU: Central Management Unit, WMU: Western Management Unit).

Table 1. Mourning Dove reporting rate (R) estimates for each State and subregion within each management unit.

Management Unit	Subregion	State	R	SE	CV
Eastern	Mid-Atlantic	Maryland	0.587	0.283	0.482
		Pennsylvania	0.431	0.142	0.329
		West Virginia	0.245	0.176	0.718
		Subregion	0.402	0.104	0.259
	South-Atlantic	North Carolina	0.751	0.159	0.212
		South Carolina	0.635	0.178	0.280
		Virginia	0.678	0.301	0.444
		Subregion	0.704	0.114	0.161
	South	Alabama	0.598	0.159	0.266
		Georgia	0.311	0.072	0.232
		Subregion	0.441	0.082	0.186
	Gulf Coast	Florida	0.538	0.170	0.316
		Louisiana	0.491	0.127	0.259
		Mississippi	0.441	0.108	0.245
		Subregion	0.446	0.071	0.160
	Mid-Central	Kentucky	0.770	0.190	0.247
		Tennessee	0.514	0.124	0.241
		Subregion	0.658	0.120	0.182
	North-West	Ohio	0.449	0.117	0.261
Central	East-South	Arkansas	0.415	0.089	0.214
		Missouri	0.624	0.138	0.221
		Subregion	0.545	0.092	0.169
	Mid-North	North Dakota	1.000	---	---
		Nebraska	1.000	---	---
		South Dakota	0.517	0.230	0.445
		Subregion	0.848	0.072	0.085
	Mid-South	Kansas	0.560	0.180	0.321
		Oklahoma	0.309	0.131	0.424
		Texas	0.316	0.070	0.222
		Subregion	0.414	0.082	0.198
Western	North-Coastal	Idaho	1.000	---	---
		Washington	0.524	0.143	0.273
		Subregion	0.772	0.068	0.089
		Arizona	0.397	0.126	0.317
		California	0.499	0.119	0.238

Table 2a. Mourning Dove adult harvest rates (H) for 2003 - 2005 in each State and subregion by management unit.

Management Unit	Subregion	State	2003 H	2003 SE	2004 H	2004 SE	2005 H	2005 SE	Total Mean	Total SE
Eastern	Mid-Atlantic	Maryland	0.065	0.036	0.085	0.043	0.085	0.040	0.078	0.023
		Pennsylvania	0.059	0.023	0.02	0.009	0.028	0.012	0.036	0.009
		West Virginia	0.033	0.015	0.047	0.036	0.027	0.023	0.036	0.015
		Subregion	0.052	0.014	0.040	0.014	0.038	0.012	0.044	0.008
	South-Atlantic	North Carolina	0.042	0.013	0.056	0.015	0.058	0.015	0.052	0.008
		South Carolina	0.075	0.024	0.072	0.024	0.041	0.013	0.063	0.012
		Virginia	0.033	0.022	0.044	0.024	0.029	0.016	0.035	0.012
		Subregion	0.049	0.010	0.058	0.011	0.048	0.009	0.052	0.006
	South	Alabama	0.083	0.029	0.06	0.021	0.050	0.018	0.064	0.013
		Georgia	0.063	0.02	0.104	0.030	0.130	0.033	0.099	0.016
		Subregion	0.072	0.017	0.084	0.019	0.094	0.020	0.083	0.011
	Gulf Coast	Florida	0.06	0.026	0.048	0.02	0.073	0.028	0.060	0.014
		Louisiana	0.117	0.041	0.075	0.031	0.045	0.018	0.079	0.018
		Mississippi	0.146	0.044	0.125	0.039	---	---	0.136	0.024
		Subregion	0.103	0.021	0.081	0.018	---	---	0.092	0.014
	Mid-Central	Kentucky	0.072	0.022	0.042	0.013	0.023	0.008	0.046	0.009
		Tennessee	0.101	0.031	0.075	0.022	0.095	0.028	0.090	0.016
		Subregion	0.085	0.018	0.056	0.012	0.054	0.013	0.065	0.009
	North-West	Ohio	0.059	0.019	0.063	0.019	0.056	0.017	0.059	0.011
		Indiana	---	---	0.122	0.037	0.097	0.031	0.110	0.016
		Wisconsin	---	---	---	---	0.074	0.031	0.074	0.031
		Subregion	---	---	---	---	0.076	0.016	0.076	0.016
Central	East-North	Iowa	0.009	0.003	0.007	0.003	0.013	0.005	0.010	0.002
	East-South	Arkansas	0.101	0.033	0.104	0.027	0.098	0.027	0.101	0.017
		Missouri	0.111	0.031	0.061	0.018	0.078	0.020	0.083	0.014
		Subregion	0.107	0.029	0.079	0.026	0.087	0.032	0.091	0.017
	Mid-North	North Dakota	0.032	0.008	0.017	0.005	0.005	0.003	0.018	0.003
		Nebraska	0.027	0.007	0.031	0.007	0.055	0.014	0.038	0.006
		South Dakota	0.037	0.013	0.042	0.011	0.012	0.008	0.030	0.006
		Subregion	0.032	0.005	0.029	0.004	0.023	0.005	0.028	0.003
	Mid-South	Kansas	0.049	0.014	0.042	0.013	0.043	0.015	0.045	0.008
		Oklahoma	0.410	0.146	0.062	0.033	0.054	0.031	0.175	0.051
		Texas	0.118	0.043	0.104	0.032	0.053	0.013	0.092	0.018
		Subregion	0.128	0.028	0.075	0.017	0.049	0.009	0.084	0.011
Western	North-Coastal	Idaho	0.038	0.012	0.017	0.006	0.017	0.006	0.024	0.005
		Washington	0.05	0.023	0.039	0.016	0.037	0.015	0.042	0.011
		Subregion	0.043	0.012	0.027	0.008	0.026	0.007	0.032	0.005
		Arizona	0.025	0.012	0.033	0.013	0.033	0.009	0.030	0.007
		California	---	---	---	---	0.204	0.042	0.204	0.042

Table 2b. Mourning Dove juvenile harvest rates (H) for 2003 - 2005 in each State and subregion by management unit.

Management Unit	Subregion	State	2003 H	2003 SE	2004 H	2004 SE	2005 H	2005 SE	Total Mean	Total SE
Eastern	Mid-Atlantic	Maryland	0.131	0.068	0.075	0.025	0.114	0.055	0.107	0.030
		Pennsylvania	0.064	0.024	0.053	0.012	0.06	0.021	0.059	0.011
		West Virginia	0.032	0.020	0.049	0.029	0.049	0.027	0.043	0.015
		Subregion	0.066	0.019	0.056	0.012	0.067	0.017	0.063	0.009
	South-Atlantic	North Carolina	0.064	0.02	0.122	0.02	0.068	0.017	0.085	0.011
		South Carolina	0.13	0.041	0.126	0.025	0.093	0.028	0.116	0.019
		Virginia	0.056	0.033	0.081	0.028	0.018	0.011	0.052	0.015
		Subregion	0.081	0.017	0.115	0.014	0.065	0.012	0.087	0.008
	South	Alabama	0.142	0.045	0.095	0.019	0.073	0.024	0.103	0.018
		Georgia	0.105	0.031	0.164	0.024	0.192	0.05	0.154	0.021
		Subregion	0.122	0.027	0.133	0.016	0.138	0.029	0.131	0.014
	Gulf Coast	Florida	0.061	0.026	0.103	0.022	0.022	0.011	0.062	0.012
		Louisiana	0.098	0.03	0.144	0.026	0.105	0.029	0.116	0.016
		Mississippi	0.169	0.051	0.122	0.022	---	---	0.146	0.023
		Subregion	0.108	0.023	0.112	0.012	---	---	0.110	0.013
	Mid-Central	Kentucky	0.059	0.018	0.068	0.013	0.037	0.012	0.055	0.008
		Tennessee	0.134	0.04	0.133	0.023	0.094	0.027	0.120	0.018
		Subregion	0.092	0.020	0.096	0.012	0.062	0.014	0.083	0.009
	North-West	Ohio	0.058	0.019	0.051	0.009	0.068	0.021	0.059	0.010
		Indiana	---	---	0.116	0.039	0.094	0.031	0.105	0.020
		Wisconsin	---	---	---	---	0.035	0.018	0.035	0.018
		Subregion	---	---	---	---	0.067	0.014	0.067	0.014
Central	East-North	Iowa	0.038	0.007	0.007	0.003	0.024	0.005	0.023	0.003
	East-South	Arkansas	0.16	0.042	0.195	0.028	0.146	0.036	0.167	0.021
		Missouri	0.119	0.034	0.106	0.018	0.172	0.043	0.132	0.019
		Subregion	0.137	0.026	0.144	0.016	0.161	0.029	0.147	0.014
	Mid-North	North Dakota	0.045	0.013	0.018	0.007	0.025	0.010	0.029	0.006
		Nebraska	0.032	0.011	0.047	0.011	0.072	0.021	0.050	0.009
		South Dakota	0.037	0.011	0.019	0.011	0.042	0.014	0.033	0.007
		Subregion	0.038	0.007	0.028	0.006	0.046	0.009	0.037	0.004
	Mid-South	Kansas	0.081	0.018	0.04	0.012	0.036	0.009	0.052	0.008
		Oklahoma	0.343	0.133	0.066	0.033	0.120	0.038	0.176	0.047
		Texas	0.118	0.044	0.061	0.013	0.069	0.018	0.083	0.016
		Subregion	0.132	0.028	0.044	0.009	0.062	0.011	0.079	0.010
Western	North-Coastal	Idaho	0.010	0.007	0.042	0.014	0.010	0.006	0.021	0.006
		Washington	0.09	0.029	0.071	0.014	0.06	0.018	0.074	0.012
		Subregion	0.046	0.014	0.055	0.010	0.032	0.009	0.044	0.006
		Arizona	0.02	0.01	0.025	0.008	0.019	0.008	0.021	0.005
		California	---	---	---	---	0.135	0.036	0.135	0.036

Table 3. Mourning Dove survival rates (S) for each State and subregion by management unit.

Management Unit	Subregion	State	Adult			Juvenile		
			S	SE	CV	S	SE	CV
Eastern	Mid-Atlantic	Maryland	0.445	0.119	0.267	0.219	0.094	0.429
		Pennsylvania	0.372	0.118	0.317	0.229	0.098	0.428
		West Virginia	0.465	0.287	0.617	0.243	0.172	0.708
		Subregion	0.407	0.110	0.271	0.232	0.078	0.336
	South-Atlantic	North Carolina	0.291	0.060	0.206	0.187	0.059	0.316
		South Carolina	0.388	0.086	0.222	0.271	0.089	0.328
		Virginia	0.690	0.229	0.332	0.244	0.137	0.561
		Subregion	0.392	0.059	0.151	0.219	0.048	0.218
	South	Alabama	0.234	0.080	0.342	0.354	0.116	0.328
		Georgia	0.284	0.059	0.208	0.261	0.065	0.249
		Subregion	0.261	0.049	0.188	0.305	0.064	0.212
	Gulf Coast	Florida	0.332	0.100	0.301	0.066	0.041	0.621
		Louisiana	0.268	0.104	0.388	0.274	0.095	0.347
		Mississippi	0.199	0.062	0.312	0.131	0.050	0.382
		Subregion	0.263	0.051	0.193	0.153	0.037	0.240
	Mid-Central	Kentucky	0.508	0.110	0.217	0.440	0.119	0.270
		Tennessee	0.265	0.063	0.238	0.184	0.059	0.321
		Subregion	0.401	0.068	0.169	0.328	0.072	0.219
	North-West	Ohio	0.400	0.080	0.200	0.145	0.046	0.317
		Indiana	0.264	0.099	0.375	0.180	0.108	0.600
		Subregion	0.328	0.064	0.196	0.163	0.061	0.373
Central	East-North	Iowa	0.732	0.251	0.343	0.333	0.165	0.495
	East-South	Arkansas	0.264	0.077	0.292	0.202	0.062	0.307
		Missouri	0.369	0.072	0.195	0.154	0.049	0.318
		Subregion	0.324	0.053	0.163	0.175	0.039	0.221
	Mid-North	North Dakota	0.452	0.192	0.425	0.425	0.240	0.565
		Nebraska	0.474	0.107	0.226	0.111	0.059	0.532
		South Dakota	0.348	0.123	0.353	0.444	0.169	0.381
		Subregion	0.427	0.087	0.204	0.329	0.104	0.316
	Mid-South	Kansas	0.495	0.105	0.212	0.407	0.121	0.297
		Oklahoma	0.563	0.322	0.572	0.475	0.229	0.482
		Texas	0.370	0.114	0.308	0.209	0.079	0.378
		Subregion	0.371	0.069	0.185	0.259	0.061	0.234
Western	North-Coastal	Idaho	0.262	0.126	0.481	0.192	0.126	0.656
		Washington	0.495	0.164	0.331	0.624	0.217	0.348
		Subregion	0.366	0.101	0.276	0.385	0.119	0.310
		Arizona	0.374	0.113	0.302	0.264	0.101	0.383

Table 4. Age-specific and pooled (All) percent distribution of Mourning Dove harvest for each banding State, 2003 - 2005.

Banding state	Recovery State or Mexico	Adult	Juvenile	Unknown	All
Alabama	Alabama	96.0	100.0	100.0	98.8
	Georgia	4.0	0.0	0.0	1.2
Arkansas	Arkansas	88.2	88.1	100.0	88.4
	Florida	1.4	0.0	0.0	0.4
	Louisiana	3.1	0.9	0.0	1.5
	Mississippi	0.0	1.3	0.0	0.9
	Mexico	0.0	1.2	0.0	0.8
	Oklahoma	4.9	4.1	0.0	4.2
	Texas	2.4	4.3	0.0	3.7
Arizona	Arizona	82.8	100.0	0.0	89.0
	California	6.9	0.0	0.0	4.4
	Mexico	10.3	0.0	0.0	6.6
California	California	100.0	92.6	100.0	96.7
	Mexico	0.0	7.4	0.0	3.3
Florida	Alabama	2.4	1.1	100.0	1.5
	Florida	95.1	97.3	0.0	96.5
	Kansas	2.5	0.0	0.0	1.0
	Missouri	0.0	1.7	0.0	0.9
Georgia	Alabama	0.7	2.8	100.0	1.9
	Georgia	99.3	96.9	0.0	97.9
	South Carolina	0.0	0.3	0.0	0.2
Iowa	Alabama	0.0	5.7	0.0	4.1
	Arkansas	7.4	0.0	0.0	1.9
	Florida	5.7	2.0	0.0	2.9
	Georgia	9.8	3.4	0.0	5.0
	Illinois	0.0	4.3	0.0	3.1
	Kansas	5.5	3.0	0.0	3.5
	Louisiana	6.2	16.3	0.0	13.3
	Maryland	0.0	1.8	0.0	1.3
	Minnesota	0.0	2.1	0.0	1.5
	Missouri	4.9	6.2	0.0	5.7
	Mississippi	12.2	4.9	0.0	3.5
	Mexico	0.0	7.5	0.0	8.5
	Nebraska	0.0	1.1	0.0	0.8
	Oklahoma	0.0	6.9	0.0	5.0
	Texas	48.3	32.6	100.0	38.3
	Unknown	0.0	2.1	0.0	1.5
Idaho	Arizona	7.7	6.9	---	7.3
	California	6.2	16.4	---	11.6
	Idaho	61.5	16.4	---	37.7
	Mexico	12.3	32.9	---	23.2
	New Mexico	0.0	5.5	---	2.9
	Oregon	12.3	11.0	---	11.6
	Utah	0.0	11.0	---	5.8
Indiana	Alabama	1.0	0.0	0.0	0.6
	Arkansas	1.5	0.0	0.0	0.9
	Georgia	2.0	0.0	0.0	1.2
	Illinois	0.0	2.2	0.0	0.8
	Indiana	90.9	91.1	100.0	91.1
	Kentucky	0.8	0.0	0.0	0.5
	Louisiana	0.0	4.4	0.0	1.6
	Ohio	0.0	2.4	0.0	0.8
	Texas	3.9	0.0	0.0	2.4

Banding state	Recovery State or Mexico	Adult	Juvenile	Unknown	All
Kansas	Arkansas	0.0	1.0	0.0	0.5
	Kansas	81.4	39.8	100.0	61.6
	Louisiana	0.0	2.1	0.0	1.0
	Missouri	3.1	4.9	0.0	3.9
	Mexico	0.0	16.2	0.0	7.8
	Oklahoma	3.2	9.6	0.0	6.2
	Texas	12.4	26.6	0.0	19.0
Kentucky	Alabama	1.7	0.0	---	0.7
	Florida	0.0	1.3	---	0.8
	Illinois	0.0	2.8	---	1.6
	Indiana	0.0	1.5	---	0.9
	Kentucky	89.2	93.7	---	91.9
	Mississippi	2.3	0.0	---	0.9
	Oklahoma	3.3	0.0	---	1.3
	South Carolina	1.6	0.0	---	0.6
	Tennessee	2.0	0.0	---	0.8
	West Virginia	0.0	0.7	---	0.4
Louisiana	Alabama	0.0	0.4	0.0	0.3
	Georgia	0.0	0.7	0.0	0.6
	Kentucky	0.0	0.3	0.0	0.3
	Louisiana	100.0	95.5	100.0	96.1
	Mississippi	0.0	1.6	0.0	1.3
	Ohio	0.0	0.5	0.0	0.4
	South Carolina	0.0	0.4	0.0	0.3
	Texas	0.0	0.7	0.0	0.6
Maryland	Delaware	0.0	7.2	0.0	4.1
	Georgia	0.0	3.9	0.0	2.2
	Maryland	90.1	85.9	42.3	86.5
	North Carolina	2.2	0.0	0.0	0.9
	Pennsylvania	7.7	0.0	57.7	4.7
	South Carolina	0.0	1.2	0.0	0.7
	Virginia	0.0	1.8	0.0	1.0
Missouri	Alabama	0.0	0.5	0.0	0.3
	Arkansas	1.2	2.3	0.0	1.7
	Florida	0.0	0.0	0.0	0.0
	Illinois	0.0	1.9	3.9	1.4
	Kansas	0.0	1.68	0.0	1.0
	Kentucky	0.7	0.8	0.0	0.7
	Louisiana	0.0	0.6	0.0	0.4
	Missouri	92.4	89.0	90.0	90.0
	Mississippi	0.0	0.3	0.0	0.2
	South Carolina	0.0	0.3	0.0	0.2
	Tennessee	1.0	0.6	0.0	0.7
	Texas	4.8	0.2	6.1	3.4
Mississippi	Alabama	2.0	1.5	0.0	1.7
	Georgia	2.0	0.0	0.0	0.8
	Louisiana	0.0	0.9	0.0	0.5
	Missouri	1.0	0.0	0.0	0.4
	Mississippi	95.0	95.8	100.0	95.5
	Tennessee	0.0	1.8	0.0	1.0
North Carolina	Georgia	0.0	1.7	0.0	1.0
	North Carolina	100.0	97.4	100.0	98.5
	South Carolina	0.0	0.9	0.0	0.5

Banding state	Recovery State or Mexico	Adult	Juvenile	Unknown	All
North Dakota	Georgia	0.0	9.3	---	4.3
	Mexico	39.7	40.5	---	40.1
	North Dakota	42.2	26.1	---	34.7
	New Mexico	0.0	5.8	---	2.7
	Texas	18.2	18.3	---	18.2
Nebraska	Kansas	0.0	5.8	---	2.5
	Mexico	1.6	28.9	---	13.5
	Nebraska	66.8	33.0	---	52.1
	Oklahoma	5.1	0.0	---	2.9
	Tennessee	3.1	0.0	---	1.7
	Texas	20.1	32.3	---	25.4
	Unknown	3.2	0.0	---	1.8
Ohio	Alabama	0.0	0.5	0.0	0.3
	Florida	0.0	0.5	0.0	0.3
	Georgia	0.0	3.2	0.0	1.7
	Louisiana	0.0	0.5	0.0	0.3
	Mississippi	1.3	0.0	0.0	0.6
	Ohio	96.7	93.3	100.0	94.9
	Pennsylvania	0.0	1.0	0.0	0.5
	South Carolina	0.9	0.0	0.0	0.4
	Tennessee	1.1	1.0	0.0	1.0
Oklahoma	Kansas	0.0	1.0	0.0	0.8
	Oklahoma	83.1	83.3	100.0	84.7
	Texas	16.9	15.7	0.0	14.6
Pennsylvania	Alabama	0.0	1.6	---	1.1
	Delaware	2.1	0.0	0.0	0.6
	Maryland	0.0	1.6	0.0	1.1
	North Carolina	0.0	1.3	0.0	0.8
	Ohio	0.0	4.1	0.0	2.8
	Pennsylvania	96.3	86.8	100.0	90.0
	South Carolina	1.6	2.2	0.0	2.0
	Tennessee	0.0	0.9	0.0	0.6
	Texas	0.0	1.5	0.0	1.0
South Carolina	Georgia	19.2	13.1	14.0	15.4
	Kentucky	1.0	0.0	0.0	0.3
	North Carolina	1.0	1.3	0.0	1.0
	South Carolina	78.8	85.6	86.0	83.3
South Dakota	Kansas	1.5	6.5	---	3.8
	Mississippi	0.0	3.9	---	1.8
	Mexico	5.8	15.4	---	10.2
	Nebraska	0.0	1.7	---	0.8
	Oklahoma	1.5	0.0	---	0.8
	South Dakota	56.3	56.6	---	56.4
	Tennessee	2.8	0.0	---	1.5
	Texas	32.2	12.5	---	23.2
	Unknown	0.0	3.4	---	1.6
Tennessee	Alabama	1.0	0.0	0.0	0.4
	Arkansas	0.0	1.0	0.0	0.6
	Florida	0.0	0.8	0.0	0.4
	Louisiana	0.0	0.9	0.0	0.5
	Missouri	0.0	0.7	0.0	0.4
	Mississippi	0.0	2.4	0.0	1.3
	Tennessee	99.0	94.3	100.0	96.4

Banding state	Recovery State or Mexico	Adult	Juvenile	Unknown	All
Texas	Alabama	0.0	1.2	0.0	0.6
	Mexico	2.8	8.5	100.0	7.0
	South Dakota	0.0	1.4	0.0	0.7
	Texas	97.2	88.9	0.0	91.8
Virginia	Virginia	100.0	100.0	100.0	100.0
Washington	Arizona	0.0	0.5	---	0.4
	California	0.0	8.0	---	7.0
	Mexico	0.0	4.5	---	3.9
	Nevada	6.5	1.0	---	1.7
	Oregon	0.0	1.0	---	0.9
	Washington	93.5	85.0	---	86.1
Wisconsin	Mississippi	12.7	0.0	---	7.6
	Texas	0.0	26.2	---	10.6
	Wisconsin	87.3	73.8	---	81.9
West Virginia	Alabama	0.0	5.4	---	3.9
	Georgia	28.3	0.0	---	7.6
	Louisiana	0.0	4.9	---	3.6
	Maryland	0.0	1.6	---	1.2
	Ohio	0.0	8.6	---	6.3
	Pennsylvania	0.0	7.5	---	5.5
	West Virginia	71.7	72.0	---	72.0

Table 5. Percent derivation by State and in Mexico of Mourning Dove adult and juvenile harvest, 2003 - 2005.

Recovery State/Mexico	Banding state	Adult	Juvenile
Alabama	Alabama	85.2	83.6
	Florida	1.5	0.6
	Georgia	2.2	5.0
	Iowa	0.0	2.6
	Indiana	3.2	0.0
	Kentucky	1.3	0.0
	Louisiana	0.0	0.3
	Missouri	0.0	0.9
	Mississippi	5.3	2.0
	Ohio	0.0	0.3
	Pennsylvania	0.0	0.3
	Tennessee	1.4	0.0
	Texas	0.0	4.3
	West Virginia	0.0	0.2
Arkansas	Arkansas	91.2	91.0
	Iowa	2.0	0.0
	Indiana	3.9	0.0
	Kansas	0.0	5.1
	Missouri	2.8	3.3
	Tennessee	0.0	0.6
Arizona	Arizona	98.9	98.2
	Idaho	1.1	1.4
	Washington	0.0	0.4
California	Arizona	1.4	0.0
	California	98.4	98.3
	Idaho	0.2	1.0
	Washington	0.0	0.7
Delaware	Maryland	0.0	100.0
	Pennsylvania	100.0	0.0
Florida	Arkansas	3.2	0.0
	Florida	93.8	94.3
	Iowa	3.0	1.9
	Kentucky	0.0	1.4
	Ohio	0.0	0.8
	Tennessee	0.0	1.6
Georgia	Alabama	1.0	0.0
	Georgia	87.1	90.0
	Iowa	0.9	0.5
	Indiana	1.7	0.0
	Louisiana	0.0	0.2
	Maryland	0.0	0.1
	Mississippi	1.4	0.0
	North Carolina	0.0	0.8
	North Dakota	0.0	2.8
	Ohio	0.0	0.5
	South Carolina	7.5	5.0
	West Virginia	0.4	0.0
Idaho	Idaho	100.0	100.0
Illinois	Iowa	0.0	20.9
	Indiana	0.0	19.9
	Kentucky	0.0	15.8
	Missouri	0.0	43.4
	North Carolina	100.0	0.0

Recovery State/Mexico	Banding state	Adult	Juvenile
Indiana	Indiana	99.6	98.9
	Kentucky	0.0	1.1
	Ohio	0.4	0.0
Kansas	Florida	0.3	0.0
	Iowa	0.3	1.0
	Kansas	98.4	84.6
	Missouri	0.0	2.1
	Nebraska	0.0	5.1
	Oklahoma	0.0	2.2
	South Dakota	1.0	4.9
Kentucky	Indiana	3.4	0.0
	Kentucky	92.2	96.3
	Louisiana	0.0	0.5
	Missouri	2.5	3.2
	South Carolina	1.9	0.0
Louisiana	Arkansas	12.8	1.7
	Iowa	6.2	7.4
	Indiana	0.0	3.1
	Kansas	0.0	5.3
	Louisiana	81.1	73.3
	Missouri	0.0	1.1
	Mississippi	0.0	1.3
	Ohio	0.0	0.4
	Tennessee	0.0	0.7
	Texas	0.0	5.3
	West Virginia	0.0	0.4
Maryland	Iowa	0.0	7.7
	Maryland	100.0	87.5
	Pennsylvania	0.0	3.0
	West Virginia	0.0	1.8
Minnesota	Iowa	---	100.0
Missouri	Florida	0.0	0.3
	Iowa	0.7	1.6
	Kansas	8.5	7.7
	Missouri	89.8	90.0
	Mississippi	1.0	0.0
	Tennessee	0.0	0.3
Mississippi	Arkansas	0.0	1.2
	Iowa	0.0	1.1
	Kentucky	0.7	0.0
	Louisiana	0.0	0.7
	Missouri	0.0	0.8
	Mississippi	95.0	93.0
	Ohio	0.4	0.0
	South Dakota	0.0	1.8
	Tennessee	0.0	1.4
	Wisconsin	4.0	0.0

Recovery State/Mexico	Banding state	Adult	Juvenile
Mexico	Arkansas	0.0	0.8
	Arizona	16.4	0.0
	California	0.0	7.2
	Iowa	2.2	3.2
	Idaho	2.0	2.1
	Kansas	0.0	20.8
	North Dakota	46.4	21.0
	Nebraska	11.3	20.5
	South Dakota	7.2	7.9
	Texas	14.4	15.7
	Washington	0.0	0.7
North Carolina	Maryland	0.2	0.0
	North Carolina	99.1	98.8
	Pennsylvania	0.0	0.2
	South Carolina	0.7	1.0
North Dakota	North Dakota	100.0	100.0
Nebraska	Nebraska	100.0	96.4
	South Dakota	0.0	3.6
New Mexico	Idaho	---	14.5
	North Dakota	---	85.5
Nevada	Washington	100.0	100.0
Ohio	Indiana	0.0	4.2
	Louisiana	0.0	0.9
	Ohio	100.0	91.7
	Pennsylvania	0.0	1.7
	West Virginia	0.0	1.5
Oklahoma	Arkansas	1.6	1.6
	Iowa	0.0	0.4
	Kansas	10.0	12.2
	Kentucky	1.2	0.0
	Nebraska	7.9	0.0
	Oklahoma	74.3	85.8
	South Dakota	5.0	0.0
Oregon	Idaho	100.0	86.0
	Washington	0.0	14.0
Pennsylvania	Maryland	6.2	0.0
	Ohio	0.0	4.7
	Pennsylvania	93.8	92.8
	West Virginia	0.0	2.5
South Carolina	Georgia	0.0	1.0
	Kentucky	1.1	0.0
	Louisiana	0.0	0.3
	Maryland	0.0	0.2
	Missouri	0.0	1.1
	North Carolina	0.0	1.1
	Ohio	0.6	0.0
	Pennsylvania	0.3	0.5
	South Carolina	98.1	95.8
South Dakota	South Dakota	100.0	90.9
	Texas	0.0	9.1

Recovery State/Mexico	Banding state	Adult	Juvenile
Tennessee	Kentucky	0.9	0.0
	Missouri	1.7	1.3
	Mississippi	0.0	2.8
	Nebraska	6.4	0.0
	Ohio	0.5	0.4
	Pennsylvania	0.0	0.2
	South Dakota	4.1	0.0
	Tennessee	86.4	95.3
Texas	Arkansas	0.2	1.1
	Iowa	0.9	1.8
	Indiana	0.8	0.0
	Kansas	5.7	10.3
	Louisiana	0.0	0.1
	Missouri	0.9	0.5
	North Dakota	3.5	1.9
	Nebraska	4.5	6.3
	Oklahoma	1.9	8.5
	Pennsylvania	0.0	0.0
	South Dakota	5.0	1.7
	Texas	76.4	67.0
	Wisconsin	0.0	0.8
Utah	Idaho		100.0
Virginia	Maryland	0.0	0.7
	Virginia	100.0	99.3
Washington	Washington	100.0	100.0
Wisconsin	Wisconsin	100.0	100.0
West Virginia	Kentucky	0.0	18.8
	West Virginia	100.0	81.2

Discussion

Study Design

Unbiased estimates of population parameters in any sample survey require that the sample be representative of the entire population. In formally designed sample surveys, this assumption is achieved by a random selection of sample units using a strict sampling protocol. For banding studies, we obviously cannot select a random sample of individual birds, but rather we rely on the assumption that our trapping design produces a representative sample from the population of interest. In this study, as in most banding studies, we employed spatial and temporal dispersion of trapping sites at larger scales and the practical field experience and local knowledge of agency biologists to achieve this objective. During the project, doves were banded in more than 330 degree blocks nationwide, most often with several individual trap sites within a degree block; thus, we believe estimates presented herein are reasonably unbiased. Specifically, we have little concern about the reporting rate estimates, because the basic sampling unit for these estimates is actually the hunter (we are measuring the hunter's reporting behavior) and not an individual dove, and there is no reason to believe that our sample of hunters was not representative. However, we do acknowledge the potential of significant bias in state harvest rate estimates if the preponderance of banding site locations was in close proximity to locations of concentrated harvest effort, or conversely, in or near suburban areas with limited harvest opportunity. We surmise this phenomenon is responsible for the exceptionally high harvest rates in a few states in a few specific years. There is a practical tradeoff between the estimation of reporting rate, in which sample size effectively increases as harvest effort increases, versus estimation of harvest rate, which depends on a sample of banded birds that is collectively representative of harvest effort in the entire state population of interest. Similar comments are relevant to estimation of survival rates, although the potential magnitude of bias is less clear because of uncertainty about the relationship between annual survival rates and harvest rates. Suffice it to say that the design of a long-term banding program spawned from this study should recognize the importance of achieving a set of banding site locations that result in a representative sample of the population, within the practical constraints of available human and fiscal resources. Consistency in banding locations over time also will help to increase statistical sensitivity to temporal changes in parameters.

We did not achieve the expected precision of $SE_{\bar{x}} = 0.05$ for subregion reporting rate estimates ($\bar{x} = 0.10$) for several reasons. Banding quotas were not achieved in some subregions. More importantly for all subregions, the *a priori* estimates of a 0.30 reporting rate (too small) and a 0.10 harvest rate (slightly too large) that were used in sample size calculations led to an underestimation of sample size required to achieve the precision goal.

Reporting Rate Comparison with Previous Studies

Tomlinson (1968) conducted the first dove reward banding study in 10 states in 1965–1966. He estimated an unweighted reporting rate of 0.32 (no variance estimate was provided) for the 10-state region, which is considerably less than the corresponding estimate of 0.55 in the present study. Reeves (1979) reported estimates of 0.31 (EMU) and 0.38 (CMU) derived from a second study during 1970 – 1972. These estimates are again considerably less than our average MU estimates of 0.53 (EMU) and 0.59 (CMU). We attribute most of this large increase to the replacement of an inscribed BBL mailing address on the band with a toll-free BBL telephone number. Annual harvest regulation publications in participating states encouraged dove hunters to look for bands, but, given the extended absence of a dove banding program, the current generation of dove hunters would not be expected to have evolved a culture of searching for and reporting bands. When Ohio conducted a reward banding study from 1996 – 1998 in coordination with the establishment of a dove hunting season in 1995, their estimated reporting rate was 0.211 (Scott et al. 2004). Their bands also did not have the toll-free number inscribed, but we surmise that inexperience in both hunting doves and reporting bands also played a role in the very low reporting rate. The estimated Ohio reporting rate in the current study was more than double the Scott et al. (2004) estimate, logically due to both the toll-free number and a more experienced hunting public.

Harvest Rate Comparison with Previous Studies

Average age-specific state harvest rate estimates derived from the large banding effort in the late 1960s and early 1970s (hereafter generically referred to as the 1970 study) have been reported by Dunks et al. (1982) for the CMU, Tomlinson et al.

(1988) for the WMU and Martin and Sauer (1993) for the EMU. Although estimation methods and assumptions were not precisely the same as those used in the current analyses, general patterns in comparisons can be informative. Current subregion harvest rate estimates for both age classes in EMU and WMU states were generally less than previous estimates, while contemporary estimates were greater or about the same as previous values in CMU states (Figs. 6a, 6b). At the MU scale, comparisons suggest an overall increase in harvest rates in the CMU, and decreases in the EMU and WMU (except CA) compared to the 1970 banding study (Fig. 7).

Survival Rate Comparison with Previous Studies

Survival rate comparisons with those from the 1970 study were not reliable at the state scale because of the poor precision of those estimates in the current study. However, precision is improved at the subregion scale, and a comparison of 2003 – 2005 age-specific estimates with those reported by Otis (2003) in his reanalysis of the 1970 banding study suggests different patterns among the management units. For the majority of age-specific comparisons in the EMU, the 1970 survival rates were greater ($\bar{x}$ difference = 0.08; Fig. 8), and simple z-test comparisons were significant (P < 0.10) for ½ of the age-specific comparisons. In the CMU, 1970 survival rates in hunting subregions were consistently greater ($\bar{x}$ difference = 0.15), and 5 of 6 age-specific comparisons were significant (P < 0.10; Fig 8b). In the non-hunting state of IA, no differences were detected. There were no significant differences between the two time periods in the relatively few comparisons in the WMU (Fig. 8b). These trends also were reflected at the MU scale (Fig. 9). Survival rates were significantly greater in 1970 for both age classes in the EMU and the CMU (P ≤ 0.10), and no differences were detected in the WMU. The EMU comparison was potentially confounded by the inclusion of the relatively large survival rates in the non-hunting New England states in the 1970 study, but the influence of these states at the MU scale was relatively small because of their relatively small dove abundance index. Both the CMU and WMU comparisons may be confounded by the missing survival rates from hunting states that did not participate in the 2003 – 2005 study, but the direction of potential bias is unknown.

Despite the several potential confounding factors inherent in comparison of current harvest distribution patterns with the 1970 banding study (heterogeneous reporting rates, different banding states, and different hunting states), the patterns are remarkably similar. The distribution of harvest in the vast majority of states is dominated by harvest in the state of banding. Exceptions were noted earlier in ID, ND, NE and SD. Dunks et al. (1982) reported the same general results for CMU states, including the exception for SD, which

accounted for about 56% of the harvest of its banded doves. During the years of their study, ND and NE were non-hunting states and thus a comparison to current results is not possible. Tomlinson et al. (1988) also reported the same patterns in the WMU, including the exception for ID, which accounted for about 35% of the harvest of its banded doves. As in the current study, Martin and Sauer (1993) reported no exceptions to the dominant contribution of in-state harvest in the EMU.

Qualitative comparisons of state harvest derivations between 1970 and 2003 – 2005 suggest that significant changes in the sources of doves harvested in a state have occurred in only a few dove hunting states. Although our results suggest that in the current study LA and TX derived relatively less of their harvest from their own breeding doves than other states, this in-state contribution was much larger than that reported for the 1970 study (LA = 45%; TX = 55%). Some of this difference can be explained by the fact that several states that contributed significantly to TX and LA harvest either did not hunt doves during the 1970 study (MI, MN, ND, NE, OH, WI) or were not banding participants in 2003 – 2005 (IL, MN). The most extreme difference is in FL, which derived only 30% of its harvest from its own breeding doves in the 1970 study. Much of this difference can be ascribed to the same factors as above, but the large difference suggests additional unknown factors may have caused an increase in the importance of the local breeding population to the FL harvest.

Management Implications

An operational nationwide banding program is critical to the implementation of an informed harvest management strategy as envisioned in the National Plan (Anonymous 2005). This study provided the initial foundation for such a program by 1) establishing field and data management protocols, 2) producing initial updated estimates of reporting, harvest, and survival rates, 3) training a new generation of biologists in dove trapping and field techniques, and 4) demonstrating a commitment by the dove management community to improved harvest management. Estimates of band reporting rates at various scales can be used to adjust future band recovery rates to obtain harvest rates, which are critical to any system of harvest management. The parameter estimates and their associated statistical precision presented herein provide a reliable empirical basis for statistical evaluation of alternative banding quotas and geographical scale of inference for an operational banding program with specific management and statistical objectives.

We believe this study provides the foundation for a long-term operational banding program that will serve several important purposes. Additional estimates of regional harvest and survival rates derived from banding data are required to construct credible population models that incorporate relationships between population status, harvest rates, harvest regulations, and management objectives. These models are integral to informed management of exploited species (Nichols et al. 1995). Second, continuous monitoring of the key population and harvest components in such a management system supports a long-term strategy of providing maximum harvest opportunity while insuring population sustainability (Williams et al. 2002) of the most harvested game bird in North America. Finally, we suggest that a long term and large scale banding program provides additional scientific value in that it generates a time series of demographic information that can be mined by investigators interested in biological, environmental, and ecological questions that are not directly related to harvest management.

Literature Cited

Anonymous. 2005. Mourning dove national strategic harvest management plan. Department of Interior, U.S. Fish and Wildlife Service, Washington, D.C.

Brownie, C., D. R. Anderson, K. P. Burnham, and D. S. Robson. 1985. Statistical inference from band recovery data – a handbook. Resource Publication 131. 2nd ed. Department of Interior, U. S. Fish and Wildlife Service, Washington D.C.

Dolton, D. D., and R. D. Rau. 2006. Mourning dove population status, 2006. Department of Interior, U. S. Fish and Wildlife Service, Laurel, Maryland,

Dunks, J. H., R. E. Tomlinson, H. M. Reeves, D. D. Dolton, C. E. Braun, and T. P. Zapatka. 1982. Migration, harvest, and population dynamics of mourning doves banded in the Central Management Unit, 1967–77. Special Scientific Report-Wildlife 249. Department of Interior, U. S. Fish and Wildlife Service, Washington, D.C.

Geis, A. D. 1972. Use of banding data in migratory game bird research and management. U.S. Bureau of Sport Fisheries and Wildlife, Special Scientific Report – Wildlife No. 154. Washington, D.C.

Hayne, D. W., and P. H. Geissler. 1977. Hunted segments of the mourning dove population: movement and importance. Southeastern Association of Game and Fish Commissioners Technical Bulletin 3.

Kiel, W. H., Jr. 1959. Mourning dove management units. U.S. Bureau of Sport Fisheries and Wildlife, Special Scientific Report –Wildlife No. 42. Washington, D.C.

Martin, F. W., and J. R. Sauer. 1993. Population characteristics and trend in the Eastern Management Unit. Pages 281–305 *in* T. S. Baskett, M. W. Sayre, R. E. Tomlinson, and R. E. Mirarchi, editors. Ecology and management of the mourning dove. Stackpole Books, Harrisburg, Pennsylvania.

Mirarchi, R. E. 1993. Sexing, ageing, and miscellaneous research techniques. Pages 399–409 *in* T. S. Baskett, M. W. Sayre, R. E. Tomlinson, and R. E. Mirarchi, editors. Ecology and management of the Mourning Dove. Stackpole Books, Harrisburg, Pennsylvania.

Munro, R. E. and C. F. Kimball. 1982. Population ecology of the mallard. VII. Distribution and derivation of the harvest. Department of Interior, U.S. Fish and Wildlife Service Resource Publication 147. Washington, D.C.

Nichols, J. D., and R. E. Tomlinson. 1993. Analyses of banding data. Pages 269–280 in T. S. Baskett, M. W. Sayre, R. E. Tomlinson, and R. E. Mirarchi, editors. Ecology and management of the mourning dove. Stackpole Books, Harrisburg, Pennsylvania.

Nichols, J. D., F. A. Johnson, and B. K. Williams. 1995. Managing North American waterfowl in the face of uncertainty. Annual Review of Ecology and Systematics 26:177–199.

Nichols, J. D., R. E. Reynolds, R. J. Blohm, R. E. Trost, J. E. Hines, and J. P. Bladen. 1995. Geographic variation in band reporting rates for mallards based on reward banding. Journal of Wildlife Management 59:697–708.

Otis, D. L. 2002. Survival models for harvest management of mourning dove populations. Journal of Wildlife Management 66:1052–1063.

Otis, D. L. 2003. A framework for reproductive models of mourning dove populations. Journal of the Iowa Academy of Science 110:13–16.

Reeves, H. M., A. D. Geis, and F. C. Kniffin. 1968. Mourning dove capture and banding. Special Scientific Report 117. Department of Interior, U. S. Fish and Wildlife Service, Washington, D.C.

Reeves, H. M. 1979. Estimates of reporting rates for mourning dove bands. Journal of Wildlife Management 43:36–42.

Sadler, K. C. 1993. Mourning dove harvest. Pages 449–459 *in* T. S. Baskett, M. W. Sayre, R. E. Tomlinson, and R. E. Mirarchi, editors. Ecology and management of the mourning dove. Stackpole Books, Harrisburg, Pennsylvania.

Scott, D. P., J. B. Berdeen, D. L. Otis, and R. L. Fendrick. 2004. Harvest parameters of urban and rural mourning doves in Ohio. Journal of Wildlife Management 68:698–700.

Schulz, J. H., S. L. Sheriff, Z. He., C. E. Braun, R. D. Drobney, R. E. Tomlinson, D. D. Dolton, and R. A. Montgomery. 1995. Accuracy of techniques used to assign mourning dove age and gender. Journal of Wildlife Management 59:759–765.

Tomlinson, R. E. 1968. Reward banding to determine reporting rate of recovered mourning dove bands. Journal of Wildlife Management 32:6–11.

Tomlinson, R. E., D. D. Dolton, H. M. Reeves, J. D. Nichols, and L. A. McKibben. 1988. Migration, harvest, and population characteristics of mourning doves banded in the Western Management Unit, 1964–77. Department of Interior, U. S. Fish and Wildlife Service Technical Report 13, Washington, D.C.

Ver Steeg, J. M., and R. C. Elden, compilers. 2002. Harvest information program: evaluation and recommendations. International Association of Fish and Wildlife Agencies, Migratory Shore and Upland Game Bird Working Group, Ad Hoc Committee on HIP, Washington, D.C.

White, G. C. 1983. Numerical estimation of survival rates from band-recovery and biotelemetry data. Journal of Wildlife Management 47:716–728.

Williams, B. K., J. D. Nichols, and M. J. Conroy. 2002. Analysis of animal populations. Academic Press, San Diego, California.

Appendix A. Number banded by State, age (A = adult, J = juvenile, U = unknown), and band type
(Code: 0 = standard, 1= standard + blank gold, 3 = standard + reward, 4 = standard, paired with reward band).

State	Age	Code	Number banded		
			2003	2004	2005
Alabama	A	0	278	390	397
		1	277	14	0
		3	0	0	0
		4	0	0	0
	J	0	288	41	594
		1	287	35	0
		3	0	212	0
		4	0	415	0
	U	0	30	3	0
		1	29	0	0
		3	0	0	0
		4	0	0	0
Alabama Total			**1189**	**1110**	**1009**
Arkansas	A	0	145	347	373
		1	145	0	0
		3	0	27	0
		4	0	66	0
	J	0	278	24	654
		1	277	0	0
		3	0	175	0
		4	0	337	0
	U	0	25	12	12
		1	24	0	0
		3	0	0	0
		4	0	0	0
Arkansas Total			**894**	**988**	**1039**
Arizona	A	0	392	641	0
		1	391	0	0
		3	0	0	296
		4	0	3	669
	J	0	362	1	0
		1	361	0	0
		3	0	265	186
		4	0	520	299
	U	0	3	10	0
		1	3	0	0
		3	0	11	4
		4	0	22	3
Arizona Total			**1512**	**1473**	**1457**
California	A	0	0	0	53
		1	0	0	0
		3	0	0	93
		4	0	0	164
	J	0	0	0	101
		1	0	0	0
		3	0	0	89
		4	0	0	190
	U	0	0	0	14
		1	0	0	0
		3	0	0	5
		4	0	0	21
California Total			**0**	**0**	**730**

State	Age	Code	Number banded		
			2003	2004	2005
Florida	A	0	195	387	358
		1	195	0	0
		3	0	0	0
		4	0	0	0
	J	0	207	0	553
		1	206	0	0
		3	0	185	0
		4	0	363	0
	U	0	6	67	41
		1	6	0	0
		3	0	0	0
		4	0	0	0
Florida Total			815	1002	952
Georgia	A	0	352	486	727
		1	352	0	0
		3	0	0	0
		4	0	1	0
	J	0	329	0	635
		1	328	0	0
		3	0	217	0
		4	0	420	0
	U	0	15	26	12
		1	14	0	0
		3	0	0	0
		4	0	0	0
Georgia Total			1390	1150	1374
Iowa	A	0	500	847	829
		1	500	0	0
		3	0	0	0
		4	0	0	0
	J	0	480	63	1248
		1	479	0	0
		3	0	462	0
		4	0	932	0
	U	0	14	21	2
		1	14	0	0
		3	0	0	0
		4	0	0	0
Iowa Total			1987	2325	2079
Idaho	A	0	118	465	519
		1	118	21	0
		3	0	0	0
		4	0	0	0
	J	0	102	30	318
		1	102	3	0
		3	0	112	0
		4	0	226	0
	U	0	4	0	2
		1	3	0	0
		3	0	0	0
		4	0	0	0
Idaho Total			447	857	839

State	Age	Code	Number banded		
			2003	2004	2005
Indiana	A	0	0	785	691
		1	0	0	0
		3	0	0	0
		4	0	0	0
	J	0	0	384	520
		1	0	0	0
		3	0	0	0
		4	0	0	0
	U	0	0	17	18
		1	0	0	0
		3	0	0	0
		4	0	0	0
Indiana Total			0	1186	1229
Kansas	A	0	350	834	395
		1	350	0	0
		3	0	0	157
		4	0	0	304
	J	0	270	0	228
		1	270	0	0
		3	0	197	105
		4	0	395	224
	U	0	4	10	3
		1	4	0	0
		3	0	0	4
		4	0	0	4
Kansas Total			1248	1436	1424
Kentucky	A	0	357	586	668
		1	356	0	0
		3	0	0	0
		4	0	0	0
	J	0	358	8	783
		1	358	0	0
		3	0	322	0
		4	0	650	0
	U	0	16	34	14
		1	16	0	0
		3	0	0	0
		4	0	0	0
Kentucky Total			1461	1600	1465
Louisiana	A	0	122	155	282
		1	121	0	0
		3	0	0	0
		4	0	0	0
	J	0	479	0	2116
		1	479	0	0
		3	0	165	0
		4	0	330	0
	U	0	39	19	41
		1	39	0	0
		3	0	0	0
		4	0	0	0
Louisiana Total			1279	669	2439

State	Age	Code	Number banded		
			2003	2004	2005
Maryland	A	0	131	195	398
		1	130	0	0
		3	0	0	0
		4	0	0	0
	J	0	104	0	289
		1	103	0	0
		3	0	96	0
		4	0	190	0
	U	0	4	12	45
		1	3	0	0
		3	0	0	0
		4	0	0	0
Maryland Total			475	493	732
Missouri	A	0	304	637	848
		1	304	0	0
		3	0	0	0
		4	0	0	0
	J	0	271	0	752
		1	271	0	0
		3	0	279	0
		4	0	556	0
	U	0	12	112	101
		1	12	0	0
		3	0	0	0
		4	0	0	0
Missouri Total			1174	1584	1701
Mississippi	A	0	257	380	323
		1	256	0	0
		3	0	0	0
		4	0	0	0
	J	0	278	0	352
		1	277	0	0
		3	0	205	0
		4	0	409	0
	U	0	2	22	6
		1	1	0	0
		3	0	0	0
		4	0	0	0
Mississippi Total			1071	1016	681
North Carolina	A	0	392	815	708
		1	392	0	0
		3	0	0	0
		4	0	0	0
	J	0	250	0	865
		1	249	0	0
		3	0	240	0
		4	0	484	0
	U	0	10	69	8
		1	9	0	0
		3	0	0	0
		4	0	0	0
North Carolina Total			1302	1608	1581

State	Age	Code	Number banded		
			2003	2004	2005
North Dakota	A	0	237	699	0
		1	237	0	0
		3	0	0	187
		4	0	1	583
	J	0	137	1	0
		1	137	0	0
		3	0	197	58
		4	0	396	244
	U	0	5	0	0
		1	5	0	0
		3	0	0	3
		4	0	0	0
North Dakota Total			758	1294	1075
Nebraska	A	0	304	656	0
		1	303	0	0
		3	0	0	146
		4	0	0	277
	J	0	148	2	0
		1	147	0	0
		3	0	190	84
		4	0	382	184
	U	0	5	8	0
		1	4	0	0
		3	0	0	1
		4	0	0	0
Nebraska Total			911	1238	692
Ohio	A	0	523	1037	997
		1	523	0	0
		3	0	0	0
		4	0	0	0
	J	0	453	26	996
		1	452	0	0
		3	0	560	0
		4	0	1123	0
	U	0	23	12	4
		1	22	0	0
		3	0	0	0
		4	0	0	0
Ohio Total			1996	2758	1997
Oklahoma	A	0	24	157	59
		1	23	0	0
		3	0	0	32
		4	0	0	61
	J	0	174	0	177
		1	174	0	0
		3	0	95	66
		4	0	195	132
	U	0	8	31	2
		1	7	0	0
		3	0	0	2
		4	0	0	7
Oklahoma Total			410	478	538

State	Age	Code	Number banded		
			2003	2004	2005
Pennsylvania	A	0	342	657	574
		1	341	0	0
		3	0	0	0
		4	0	0	0
	J	0	420	0	1077
		1	420	0	0
		3	0	304	0
		4	0	612	0
	U	0	23	77	40
		1	23	0	0
		3	0	0	0
		4	0	0	0
Pennsylvania Total			1569	1650	1691
South Carolina	A	0	319	368	838
		1	318	0	0
		3	0	0	0
		4	0	0	0
	J	0	202	0	643
		1	202	0	0
		3	0	162	0
		4	0	333	0
	U	0	141	128	194
		1	141	0	0
		3	0	0	0
		4	0	0	0
South Carolina Total			1323	991	1675
South Dakota	A	0	413	701	46
		1	413	0	45
		3	0	0	131
		4	0	0	218
	J	0	337	0	54
		1	337	0	55
		3	0	198	86
		4	0	397	214
	U	0	0	0	0
		1	0	0	0
		3	0	0	0
		4	0	0	0
South Dakota Total			1500	1296	849
Tennessee	A	0	238	620	441
		1	237	0	0
		3	0	0	0
		4	0	0	0
	J	0	222	0	712
		1	222	0	0
		3	0	199	0
		4	0	395	0
	U	0	54	170	36
		1	54	0	0
		3	0	0	0
		4	0	0	0
Tennessee Total			1027	1384	1189

State	Age	Code	Number banded		
			2003	2004	2005
Texas	A	0	252	557	0
		1	251	0	0
		3	0	0	176
		4	0	0	345
	J	0	226	3	0
		1	225	0	0
		3	0	281	150
		4	0	565	303
	U	0	6	22	0
		1	6	0	0
		3	0	0	3
		4	0	0	12
Texas Total			966	1428	989
Virginia	A	0	114	262	306
		1	113	0	0
		3	0	0	0
		4	0	0	0
	J	0	122	0	503
		1	122	0	0
		3	0	91	0
		4	0	176	0
	U	0	2	12	10
		1	2	0	0
		3	0	0	0
		4	0	0	0
Virginia Total			475	541	819
Washington	A	0	126	237	215
		1	126	0	0
		3	0	0	0
		4	0	0	0
	J	0	329	0	1033
		1	328	0	0
		3	0	276	0
		4	0	558	0
	U	0	5	15	8
		1	5	0	0
		3	0	0	0
		4	0	0	0
Washington Total			919	1086	1256
Wisconsin	A	0	0	0	238
		1	0	0	0
		3	0	0	0
		4	0	0	0
	J	0	0	0	321
		1	0	0	0
		3	0	0	0
		4	0	0	0
	U	0	0	0	11
		1	0	0	0
		3	0	0	0
		4	0	0	0
Wisconsin Total			0	0	570

State	Age	Code	Number banded		
			2003	2004	2005
West Virginia	A	0	98	261	153
		1	98	0	0
		3	0	0	0
		4	0	0	0
	J	0	246	0	471
		1	245	0	0
		3	0	163	0
		4	0	332	0
	U	0	7	10	5
		1	6	0	0
		3	0	0	0
		4	0	0	0
West Virginia Total			**700**	**766**	**629**
All States Total			28,798	33,408	34,700

Appendix B. Total number of recoveries in 2003-2005 in banding States, age (A = adult, J = juvenile, U = unknown), and band type (Code: 0 = standard, 1= standard + blank gold, 3 = standard + reward, 4 = standard, paired with reward band).

State	Age	Code			
		0	1	3	4
Alabama	A	42	13	0	0
	J	59	24	24	26
	U	2	1	0	0
Arkansas	A	50	12	3	1
	J	63	38	38	33
	U	2	4	0	0
Arizona	A	18	12	8	12
	J	5	7	14	9
	U	0	0	0	0
California	A	3	0	19	20
	J	9	0	12	12
	U	0	0	1	1
Florida	A	37	11	0	0
	J	11	12	20	20
	U	4	1	0	0
Georgia	A	65	30	0	0
	J	65	27	43	29
	U	3	2	0	0
Iowa	A	17	6	0	0
	J	22	10	18	6
	U	1	2	0	0
Idaho	A	21	8	0	0
	J	5	5	5	7
	U	0	0	0	0
Indiana	A	82	0	0	0
	J	45	0	0	0
	U	1	0	0	0
Kansas	A	55	15	3	7
	J	11	18	17	18
	U	2	0	0	0
Kentucky	A	63	34	0	0
	J	40	33	23	42
	U	2	0	0	0
Louisiana	A	19	19	0	0
	J	137	57	25	28
	U	7	0	0	0
Maryland	A	39	11	0	0
	J	29	9	9	10
	U	2	1	0	0
Missouri	A	218	31	0	0
	J	233	31	34	44
	U	33	1	0	0
Mississippi	A	45	47	0	0
	J	23	54	29	26
	U	2	0	0	0
North Carolina	A	93	23	0	0
	J	65	13	32	47

State	Age	Code			
		0	1	3	4
	U	5	3	0	0
North Dakota	A	22	5	2	1
	J	4	4	4	10
	U	0	0	0	0
Nebraska	A	41	13	6	13
	J	3	4	8	19
	U	0	0	0	0
Ohio	A	76	32	0	0
	J	43	19	33	25
	U	1	0	0	0
Oklahoma	A	7	5	2	1
	J	24	27	12	10
	U	3	3	0	0
Pennsylvania	A	33	19	0	0
	J	52	23	18	21
	U	5	0	0	0
South Carolina	A	63	36	0	0
	J	54	33	19	34
	U	26	11	0	0
South Dakota	A	24	11	4	2
	J	11	10	14	8
	U	0	0	0	0
Tennessee	A	72	27	0	0
	J	55	29	30	32
	U	10	4	0	0
Texas	A	29	18	12	5
	J	14	9	28	21
	U	0	0	0	1
Virginia	A	25	4	0	0
	J	10	7	8	11
	U	1	0	0	0
Washington	A	17	7	0	0
	J	57	30	26	26
	U	0	0	0	0
Wisconsin	A	8	0	0	0
	J	5	0	0	0
	U	0	0	0	0
West Virginia	A	9	0	0	0
	J	9	6	8	5
	U	0	0	0	0
Total		**2,568**	**1,022**	**614**	**647**

Appendix C. Participating state banding coordinators and staff.

Acknowledgements of contributions of field and support staff in cooperating banding states, 2003 - 2005. State wildlife agency coordinators are listed first.

Alabama

Jeff Makemson; Alabama Department of Conservation and Natural Resources

Brett Abbott, Frank Allen, Steve Bryant, Tony Burgett, Gene Carver, Thagard Colvin, Chris Cook, Ben Davis, Ron Eakes, Jud Easterwood, Joel Glover, Stewart Goldsby, Dr. Barry Grand, Wendell Hallman, Andy Hughes, Chris Jaworowski, Wayne Kelly, Randy Liles, Jeff Makemson, Mitchell Marks, James Masek, Chad Masley, Ray Metzler, Phil Miller, Chas Moore, Bennett Moseley, Tracy Nelson, Erica Nix, Adam Pritchett, Kevin Pugh, Jim Schrenkel, Richard Tharp, Crystal Tindell, Bruce Todd, Daniel Toole, Myron Wiley

Arizona

Mike Rabe; Arizona Game and Fish Department

Contributing staff of the Arizona Game and Fish Department

Arkansas

Mike Checkett, Andrew James; Arkansas Game and Fish Commission

Mark Barbee, Mark Hooks, Roger Milligan, Rusty Mitchell, Allen Clawson, Roger Theis, Andy VanHorn, David Luker, Alton Case, Ruth Chapman, Jason Carbaugh, James Foster, Shaun Merrell, Paul Provence, Kent Wagner, Rick Darter, John Gallagher, Terry Gentry, Brian Infield, Kevin Lynch, Nicole Peterson, Eley Talley, Gregg Mathis, Mickey Rogers, Griffin Park, Brad Townsend, Cameron Tatom, Terry Rogers, George Howell, Mike Harris, Charles Self, Steven Fowler, Mike Morman, Susan Gregory, Scotty Winningham, Brady Baker, Lee Kirkpatrick, Jeremy Self, Hilda Jones, Chris Carter, Matt Mourot, Kenny Vernon, Bobby Conley, Mike Widner, Johnny Waldrup, Roger Martin, Josh Fortner, Don Curran, Ritchie Bryant, Wayne Kelley, Danny Denney, Dustin Davis, Deanne Taylor, Jenna Roy, Jacob Bokker

California

Tom Blankinship, Pat Lauridson; California Department of Fish and Game

Contributing staff of the California Department of Fish and Game

Florida

Kurt Hodges; Florida Fish and Wildlife Conservation Commission

Jim Alleman, John Ault, Ashleigh Blackford, Pam Boody, Joseph Bozzo, Dan Buchanan, Nathan Bunting, Dan Castillo, Brian Christ, Jean - Marie Conner, Neal Franklin Eichholz, Jamie Feddersen, Norberto Fernandez, Don Francis, Derek Fussell, Kelly Gamble, Cyndi Gates, Wesley Gates, Allan Hallman, Tina Hannon, Sharon Hester, Tommy C. Hines, Beth Hodges, Kurt Hodges, Andrew Jernigan, Russell Johnson, Curt Kleist, Paige Martin, Daniel McDonald, David McDuffie, Jeff McGrady, Chuck McKelvy, Mike McMillian, Jennifer Morse, Tim O'Meara, Melissa Peagler, Annemarie Prince, Tim Regan, Royce A. Schneider, Paul Schulz, James Schuette, Billy Sermons, Wynne Sermons, Roger Shields, Tom Shupe, Donald R. Smith, Phillip E. Smith, Valerie Sparling, Lee Taylor, Jason Williams

Georgia

Don McGowan; Georgia Department of Natural Resources

Contributing staff of the Georgia Department of Natural Resources

Idaho

Tom Hemker; Idaho Department of Fish and Game

Contributing staff of the Idaho Department of Fish and Game

Indiana

Jim Pitman; Indiana Department of Natural Resources

Larry Allsop, Steve Backs, Fred Bebout, Mark Bennett, Jim Bergens, Matthew Bredeweg, Tony Carroll, John Castrale, Tom Despot, Brad Detamore, Shauna Dollinger, Brad Feaster, John Gibson, Jason Gilbert, Josh Griffin, Kent Hanauer, Bill Hardin, Sterling Hartzog, Donald Hast, Michael Holcomb, Greg Leer, Mel Lehmer, Nate Levitte, Glenn McCormick, Scott McCormick, Heidi McDonald, Randy Millar, Steve Mund, Danny Orr, Dave Parker, Rick Peercy, Adam Phelps, Jim Pitman, Bruce Plowman, Mark Pochon, Ron Ronk, Steve Roth, Michael Schoof, Mike Schoonveld, Phillip Sewell, Ray Shepard, Dave Spitznagle, Roger Stonebraker, Rob Sullender, Jeff Thompson, Alger van Hoey, Jason Wade, Bev Wagner, Jon Weber, Sam Whiteleather, Dennis Workman, Jim Young

Iowa

Todd Bogenschutz; Iowa Department of Natural Resources

Angie Auel, Jason Auel, Brandon Burrows, Doug Chafa, Justin Clark, Richard Coy, Jackie Dollinger, Steve Espeland, Farmer, Jerry, Goodrich, Kevin, Mike Griffin, Jason Gritsch, Terry Hainfield, Matt Handy, Greg Hanson, James D. Hanson, Bryan Hellyer, T. J. Herrick, Pete Hildreth, Ron Howing, Doug Janke, Nick Jordan, Chuck Kakac, Curt Kemmerer, Mike Klein, Vickie Klein, Calvin Kunkle,

Dave Kutz, Chris LaRue, Mike Mahn, Corey Meyer, Ron Munkel, Dean Nelson, Bill Ohde, George Olson (temp), Jessica Parkhurst, Chad Paup, Ike Petersen, Scott Peterson, Doug Phillips, Carl Priebe, Rene Richter, Andy Robbins, Jonathan Ross, Greg L. Schmitt, Tom Smith, Wayne Souer, Chuck Steffen, Jeff Telleen, Brett Tevine, Tim Thompson, Casey Trine, Rick Trine, Chris Vandello, Dave Vanderpluym, Ed Weiner, David White, Ed White, Ryan White, Steve Woodruff

Kansas
Helen Hands; Kansas Department of Wildlife and Parks

Edward Aeschliman, Aaron Austin, Clint Bowman, Gene Brehm, Philip Buser, Lee Callens, Andy Friesen, Todd Gatton, Helen Hands, John Hoke, Jerry Horak, Karl Karrow, Craig Kennedy, Marvin Kraft, Lucas Kramer, Toby Marlier, Brian Miewes, Kelly Miller, Tom Norman, Mike Nyhoff, Ricky Ochoa, Angie Owensby, Rob Penner, Keith Reif, Brad Rueshhoff, Ron Ruthstrom, Matt Schoshke, Kathy Sexson, Mark Sexson, Andrea Smith, Dwight Spencer, Hiram Thoman, Tyler Thomasson, Kirk Thompson, Manuel Torres, Roxanna Tosterud

Kentucky
Rocky Pritchart, Beth Cuzio; Kentucky Department of Fish and Wildlife Resources

Herbie Adams, John Akers, Bill Balda, Steve Beam, Tony Black, Dennis Boggs, Steven Bonney, Pat Brandon, Earl Brown, Gerald Burnett, Josh Burton, Scott Buser, Oliver Capps, Leslie Carter, Brian Clark, Buford Clark, Robert Colvis, Lee Cope, George Corder, Dan Crank, Elizabeth Cuzio, Larry Dennis, Dana Dolen, Tom Edwards, Joyce Fitzgerald, Scott Friedhoff, Chris Garland, Chris Grasch, Brian Gray, Nathan Gregory, Brian Grossman, Rusty Hamilton, Mark Harless, Scott Harp, Mike Henshaw, Wes Hodges, Greg Isen, Rene Jimenez, Tim Kreher, Joe Lacefield, Jim Lane, Bill Lisowski, Rebecca Littleton, Bill Lynch, Dale Lynch, Chris Mason, Wes Mattox, Rick Mauro, David McChesney, Jason McDowell, Steve McMillen, Bobby Morse, Mike Morton, Cecil Parish, Pat Pierce, Jayson Plaxico, Rocky Pritchert, Bill Ridner, Dave Ross, Marsha Schroder, Phil Sharp, Jack Sloan, Brian Smith, Clay Smitson, Tim Stoval, Wayne Tamminga, Kim Tarter, Kevin Tucker, Brian Wagner, Martin Wheeldon, Charlie Wilkins, Eric Williams

Louisiana
Mike Olinde; Louisiana Department of Wildlife and Fisheries

Barrett Arthur, Brannon Arthur, Hugh Arthur, Chuck Bantel, Leonard Bennett, Charlie Booth, Edwin Bordelon, Francis Bordelon, Johnathan Bordelon, David Breithaupt, Cecil Brookin, Tommy Bruhl, Bill Burns, Don Carpenter, Sammie Cerami, Perry Corbett, Greg Crawford, Pat Deshotels, Travis Dufour, Jeffery Dupuy, Robert Marty

Edmunds, Jimmy Ernst, Randy Ewing, Jason Frost, Duffy Guillory, Scott Halphen, John Hanks, David Hayden, Mike Hollier, Jarrod Hughes, Barrett Kiser, Bruce Knight, Gregory Lachney, Glenn Lee, Ryan Lemoine, Danny Lively, Richard McMullan, Lowrey Moak, Randy Myers, CR Newland, Ben Oubre, Jerald Owens, Guy Patout, Donald Phillips, Mike Pirot, Elbert Rachal, John Robinette, Mark Roy, Wendell Smith, Shanon Soileau, Justin Sonnier, Kerney Sonnier, Jimmy Stafford, Jeff Taylor, Jr., Errol Theriot, Chad Thomas, Clyde Thompson, Adam Trevillion, Tony Vidrine, Larry Waldron, Mac Ware, Johnny Warren, Calvin Waskom, Tom Woods, Reggie Wycoff

Maryland
Bill Harvey; Maryland Department of Natural Resources

Jose Alachan, Patty Allen, Pete Bendel, Jim Bennett, James Bowling, Danny Callahan, Ed Cook, Brent Evans, Brian Eyler, Fritz Faust, Richard Garrett, Dennis Hammett, Bill Harvey, Dave Heilmeier, Josh Homyack, Mark Hooper, Tyler Johnson, Carla Johnson, Barbara Joyce, Ernie Licalzi, Bob Long, Bill Martin, Ron Norris, Keri Parker, Scott Peters, Denny Price, Rebecca Rau,Frank Ryan, Greg Schenck, Hutch Walbridge, Donald Webster

Mississippi
Dave Godwin; Mississippi Department of Wildlife, Fisheries and Parks

Kevin Brunke, Chris Clark, Scott Edwards, Dave Godwin, John Gruchy, Rob Heflin Jr., Brad Holder, Kathy Shelton, Roger Tankesly, Jim Willcutt

Missouri
John Schulz; Missouri Department of Conservation

Barry Allen, Josh Banks, Jamie Barton, Wade Bealmer, Reggie Bennett, Ted Bond, Jason Braunecker, Rick Bredesen, Mike Brillhart, Dennis Browning, Joe Bruno, Deb Burns, Shane Bush, Rob Chapman, Chris Cole, Kendall Coleman, Terry Coon, Craig Crisler, Chase Curtis, Kathy DeiSanti, Bill Dent, Jason Dungan, Ashley Dunkle, Dave Erickson, Matt Fenoff, Jason Gargus, John George, Norb Giessman, Nick Girondo, Jeff Goin, Nick Hartman, Josh Heintz, Bob Henry, Jerod Heubner, Lee Hughes, Todd Hunt, Mark Hutchings, Tim James, Dustin Johnson, Mike Jones, Brad Jump, Ryan Kelly, Ryan Kelly, Steve Kistner, Cesare Kleeman, Ashleigh Klingman, Drew Larsen, Tom Leifield, Frank Loncarich, Jim Loveless, Rick McClellan, Monte McQuillen, Doreen Mengel, Mitch Miller, Chase Miller, Tony Mong, Shellie Murril, Debbie Newton, Eric Niemeyer, Carolyn Polston, Joel Porath, Cole Prenger, Ken Rampley, Jamie Reynolds, Larry Rieken, Mitch Roberts, Kristine Ruegge, Christi Ruegge, Tim Russel, Jimmy Ryder, Mike Schroer, Abby Schultz, Jeff Scott, Jessica Shaffer, Matt Smith, Rachael Stark, Jay Steele, Andy Sterling, Preston Stogsdill, Dave Stroppel, Brad Swank, Jackie Sweeney, Mark

Switzer, Andy Tappmeyer, Josh Terhune, Steve Theiss, Gene Toombs, Dirac Twidwell, Dave Urich, Rob Vinson, Tyler Warner, Harriet Weger, Brad Wessel, Beau White, Allyson Wiegman, Darrin Wood

Nebraska
Scott Taylor; Nebraska Game and Parks Commission

Mick Bresley, Mark Feeney, Russ Hamer, Kirk Hansen, Travis Kopf, Mike Remund, Warren Schwanebeck, Brad Seitz, Chad Taylor

North Carolina
Dennis Luszcz, Joe Fuller; North Carolina Wildlife Resources Commission

Chip Alexander, Brad Allen, Jason Allen, Chris Baranski, Don Barker, Daron Barnes, Denton Baumbarger, Brent Beamer, Brady Beck, Carl Betsill, Eli Beverly, Joe Blastick, Mike Carraway, Richard Clark, David Cobb, Josh Copenhaver, Jason Creegan, Lee Criscoe, Andy Davis, Dale Davis, Mark Dover, Bill Edwards, Jennifer Edwards, Pat Farrell, Joe Folta, Vic French, Joe Fuller, Michael Greene, Brad Gunn, Harlan Hall, Bronson Hannah, Greg Hochstetler, Brad Howard, Doug Howell, Tommy Hughes, Adam Johnson, Mark Jones, Steve Juhan, Jim Keepfer, Tim Keller, Ken Knight, Drew Larson, Mike Legare, Dennis Luszcz, Jeff Marcus, Dan Martin, Kimberly McCargo, Scott McLean, Brandon Minor, Andrew Mynatt, Deanna Noble, Robbie Norville, Wib Owen, Thomas Padgett, Adrienne Paoletta, Bill Parsons, Don Riley, Johnny Riley, Lincoln Sadler, Ron Sanders, Ken Shughart, Brian Smith, David Stewart, Phil Stone, George Strader, Benjy Strope, Perry Sumner, Chris Teague, Michael Tipton, Chris Turner, Tony Wait, Mark Williams, Matt Williams, Paul Williams, Tony Woolard, Justin Yale

North Dakota
Stan Kohn, Mike Szymanski; North Dakota Game and Fish Department

Bismarck NDGF, Devils Lake NDGF, Dickinson NDGF, Jamestown NDGF, Lonetree WMA, Riverdale NDGF, Arrowwood NWR, Crosby WMD, J. Clark Salyer NWR, Long Lake NWR, Lake Ilo NWR, Tewaukon NWR, Upper Souris NWR, Audubon NWR, Chase Lake WMD, Lake Alice NWR, SW BLM - Dickinson

Ohio
Dave Scott, Scott Hull; Ohio Department of Natural Resources

John Abele, Ron Adams, Brett Beatty, Bruce Buckingham, Scott Butterworth, Ron Carter, Matt Conner, Tim Davis, Fred Dierkes, Rick Dorn, Steve Douglas, Jim Duckworth, Terry Eberling, R. Lyle Fendrick, Ron Ferenchak, Sean Finke, Bob Ford, Tyler Frysinger, Kathy Garza-Behr, Beth Geboy, Rich Geboy, Damon Greer, Joe Hassman, Kevin Higgins, Doug Hissong, Dan Hollenbaugh, Dave

Honeycutt, Ryan Jackson, Jeff Janosik, Laura Jenkins, Harry Keeney, Jason Keller, Kelley Kelley, Bryan Kichta, Dave Kohler, Melissa Lackey, Andy Landon, Al Lea, Jason Leach, Erik Lewis, Lindsay Linkhart, Eric Long, John Matthews, Carla Maxwell, Stephen Menno, Randy Morgan, John Morton, Julia Murgatroyd, Ross Muszynski, Kristin Mylecraine, John Neider, Karen Norris, Lou Orosz, Mike Parker, Scott Phillips, Jessica Piispanen, Jeff Porter, Nicholas Ray, Mike Reynolds, Dale Riehle, Dave Risley, Aaron Robinson, George Saksa, Dave Scott, Chris Smith, Vern Snyder, Dennis Solon, Nathan Stricker, Andy Thompson, Andrea Tibbels, Michael White, Gretchen White, Chris Witmer, Mark Witt, Eli Young, James Young, Mike Zaleski

Oklahoma
Mike O'Meilia; Oklahoma Department of Wildlife Conservation

Robert Guinn, Lewis Jennings, Jeff Neal, Mike O'Meilia, Scott Parry, Jeff Pennington, Thad Potts, John Ridge, Kelvin Schoonover, Mark Shurden, Mike White

Pennsylvania
John Dunn; Pennsylvania Game Commission

Elizabeth Ball, Arthur Brunst, Mary Jo Casalena, James Domire, John Dunn, Susan Ellis, Jack Gilbert, Jennifer Gillis, Ian Gregg, Dave Griffin, Bruce Guinter, Robert Hodge, Kevin Jacobs, Skip Lamoreaux, Tracey Librandi-Mumma, Mike McMenamin, John Morgan, Keith Mullin, William Palmer, Amber Rendulic, Matt Roberts, Chris Rosenberry, Tony Ross, Kyle Russel, Keith Sanford, John Sites, Jeremy Stempka, Cary Stultz

South Carolina
Billy Dukes; South Carolina Department of Natural Resources

Keenan Adams, Roy Atkinson, Buddy Baker, Judy Barnes, Dave Baumann, Jeff Baumann, Daniel Beach, Greg Boling, Ryan Bowles, Jay Butfiloski, Jay Cantrell, Will Carlisle, Patty Castine, Ross Catterton, Mike Caudell, Sam Chappelear, Clemson University, Damon Gun Club, Edwin Dargan, Billy Dukes, Ben Duncan, Kell Fitts, Billy Fleming, Ron Fleming, Joyce Foster, Bernie Good, Jane Griess, Tom Harkins, Dean Harrigal, John Hoffman, Chris Holcombe, Nate Holmes, Michael Hook, Bob Hortman, Laura Housh, Mike Housh, Greg Hudson, Tim Ivey, Kevin Jarrell, Brian Kaminskas, Jim Killian, Scott Lanier, Jim Lee, Jeremy Lemacks, James Ling, Larry Lollis, Joe Lucas, David Lynch, Bill Mace, Bill Mahan, Erik Martin, Doug Mason, Kay McCutcheon, Tarri McKinney, Medway Plantation, Ben Miller, Jamie Mills, Gerald Moore, Richard Morton, Mulberry Plantation, Jim Mullis, Mark Parker, Bobby Pearson, Dewey Petty, Jason Plemmons, Stuart Plowden, Mark Purcell, Jeff Quick, Ted Rainwater, Walt Rhodes, Charles Ruth, T. J. Savereno, Mike Scales, Derrell Shipes, Elliott Shuler, Willie Simmons, Matt Smoak, South Carolina

Forestry Commission, Gary Stephens, Sam Stokes, Jr., Donnie Stone, Tommy Strange, Travis Sumner, Tom Swayngham, David Tant, Swinton Thomas, Elizabeth Vaughn, Mike Vaughn, Lisa Walters, Clay Ware, Steven Welch, Jim Westerhold, Jeff Witt, Bryan Woodward, Larry Woodward

South Dakota
Paul Mammenga; South Dakota Department of Game, Fish and Parks

Doug Alvine, Bob Curtis, Curt Dagel, Ron Fowler, Mark Grovijahn, Corey Huxoll, Tom Kirschenmann, Tony Leif, Andy Lindbloom, Paul Mammenga, Owen Mcelroy, Will Morlock, Ron Schauer, Art Smith, Chad Switzer, Spencer Vaa, George Vandel, Loren Vande Stroet, Lorene Wasland, Greg Wolbrink

Tennessee
Tim White; Tennessee Wildlife Resources Agency

George Buttrey, Jack Colwick, Randy Cromer, Ben Layton, Larry Marcum, Don Orr, Steve Patrick, Ron Saunders, Robert Smith, Ken Smith, Stacy Stevenson

Texas
Jay Roberson; Texas Parks and Wildlife Department

Bill Adams, Ty Bartoskewitz, Jason Brooks, Jose Cano, Suzanne Contreras, Steven Cortez, Philip Dickerson, James Edwards, Jason Ford, Randy Fugate, Jim Gallagher, Lauri Heintz, Joe Herrera, Sara Herrera, Mike Janis, Rick Knipe, Kevin Kriegel, Daniel Kunz, Billy Lambert, Wes Littrell, Duane Lucia, Evan McCoy, Krista McDermid, Todd Merendino, Chris Mostyn, Charlie Newberry, Todd Pilcik, Nathan Rains, Calvin Richardson, Jay Roberson, Chip Ruthven, Jimmy Rutledge, Dale Schmidt, T. Wayne Schwertner, Raymond Sims, David Sierra, David Synatzske, Trevor Tanner, Gary Waggerman, Roy Welch, Brian Wheat, Jay Whiteside, Dana Wright

Virginia
Gary Costanzo; Virginia Department of Game and Inland Fisheries

Contributing staff of the Virginia Department of Game and Inland Fisheries

Washington
Ron Friesz; Washington Department of Fish and Wildlife

Dana Base, Jeff Bernatowicz, Martin Ellenburg, Pat Fowler, Ron Friesz, Marc Hallet, Eric Holman, Don Kraege, Mike Livingston, Tom McCall, Warren Michaelis, Paul Wik

West Virginia
Steve Wilson; West Virginia Division of Natural Resources

David Arbogast, Larry Berry, Colin Carpenter, James Craft, Tom Dotson, Gary Foster, Shawn Head, William Igo, David McClung, Jeff McCrady, Patty Morrison, Allan Niederberger, Mike Peters, Steve Rauch, Eric Richmond, Rich Roger, Gary Sharp, Kem Shaw, Tammy Shreve, Bob Smith, Lee Strawn, Gary Strawn, Clarence Williamson, Steve Wilson

Wisconsin
Kent Van Horn; Wisconsin Department of Natural Resources

Kimberlee Benton, Brian Buenzow, Robert Cartegena, ChuckGatling, Brian Glenzinski, Erin Grossman, Heidi Hayes, Steve Hoffman, Jeremy Holtz, Jim Holzwart, Marty Johnson, Rich Kahl, Pat Kaiser, Dale Katsma, Renee Kerska, Charlie Kilian, Steve Klock, Craig Kopacek, Sayer Larson, Eric Lobner, Tanya Meives, Dick Nikolai, Allison Oberc, Al Ramminger, Jerry Reetz, Paul Samerdyke, Missy Sparrow-Lien, Jim Tomasko, Kent Van Horn, Larry Vine, Dan Weidert.

www.ingramcontent.com/pod-product-compliance
Lightning Source LLC
Chambersburg PA
CBHW060531010626
45794CB00023B/3309